Quilting

from little things...

Sarah Fielke

Quilting
from little things...

MURDOCH BOOKS

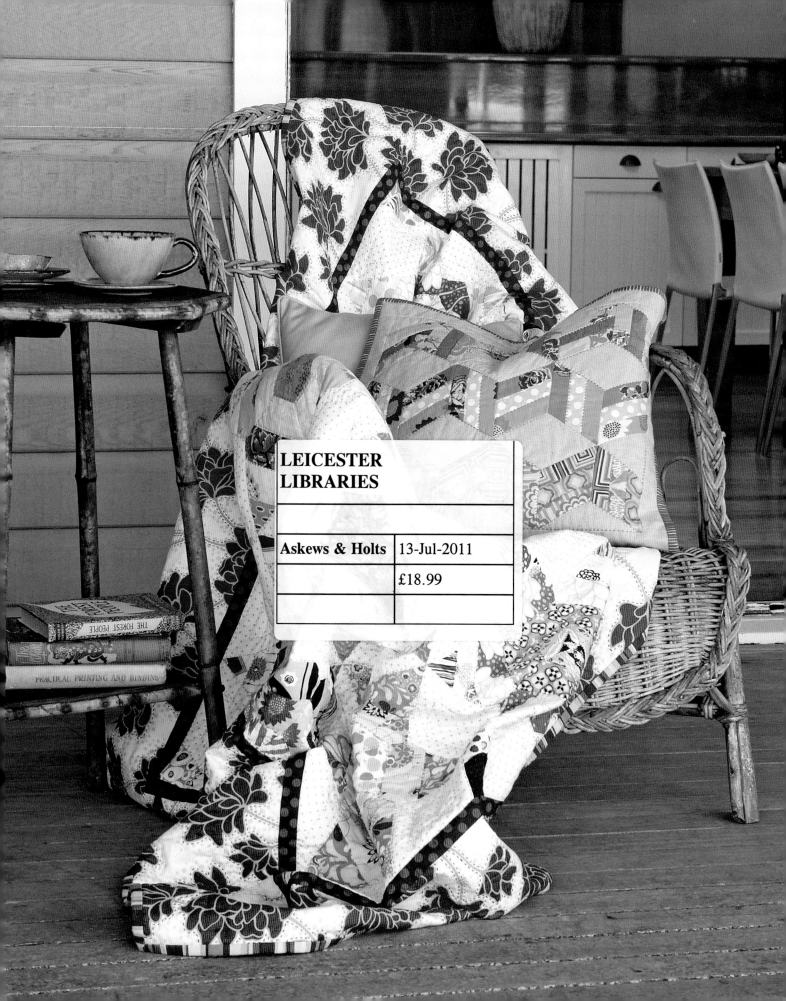

Contents

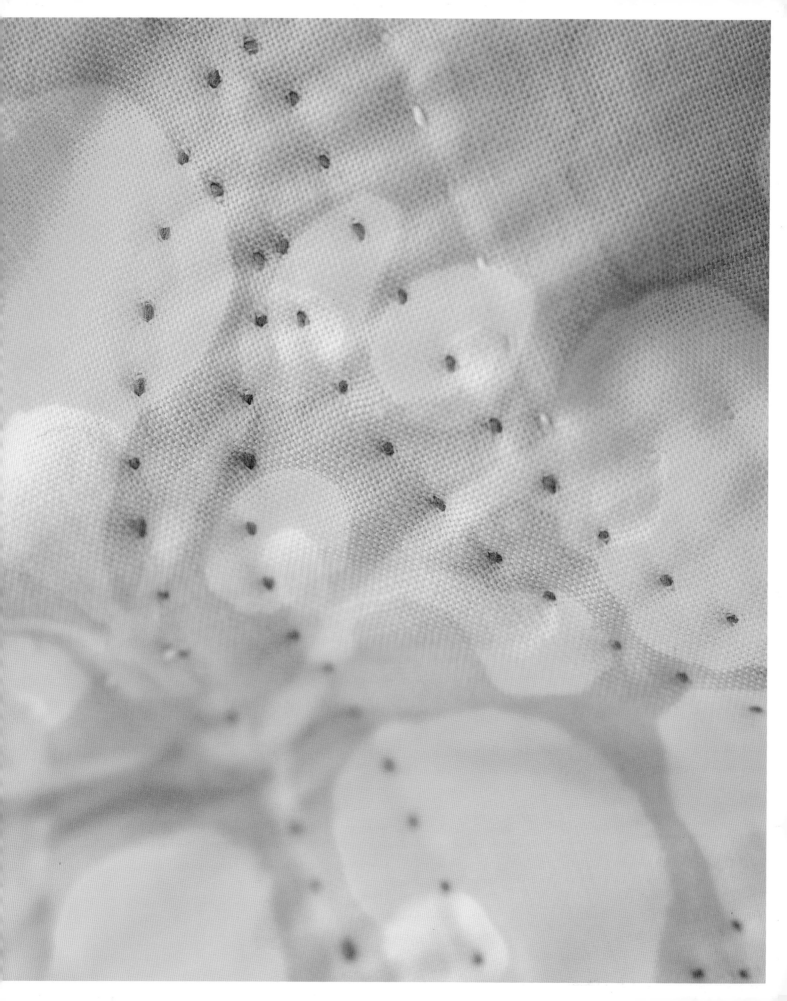

Introduction

Writing this book and designing and making the quilts that are in it has been the biggest adventure I have ever had.

They say that from little things, big things grow. When I started my new little business at the beginning of 2010, I wondered just what I would be able to grow from it. It was a leap of faith to leave my previous business partnership, Material Obsession, and begin again on my own... but things are growing and putting down roots everywhere I look, and life is very exciting!

I have written two quilt books before this one and also written articles for magazines. But writing this book has meant deciding on what my own personal style really is, distilling it and applying it liberally to anything that came into contact with the creation of *Quilting*.

To find just what that style is, I needed a huge amount of self-examination, and also examination of my quilts: what I like and don't like about them; why I made them; and what I think works and doesn't work about them. Doing all this and sticking with what I found has required a lot of discipline and focus.

Why am I telling you all this? Because every quilt you make should be an adventure, and every new project should be a project in self-awareness and discovery.

Let's not get too highbrow here, though. I don't expect that all of you are going to go out and reinvent your quilting lives because I tell you to. What I do hope you take from this book, however, is the courage to try something different, to experiment with techniques, colours or textures that you may not have tried before, and discover what inspires, fulfils and delights you about the quilts that you make.

The pairs of quilts in this book are designed to be like little lessons, although you certainly don't have to use them that way. Each pair is a dolly (or small) quilt, and a larger quilt to go with it. The pair of quilts uses the same technique to arrive at a finished product. The idea is that if you have not tried a technique before, you can make the small quilt first as a tester, to see whether the style of working suits you. That way, you can

Every new project you start should be a project in self-awareness and discovery

expand your skill base without committing to a big bed quilt every time. From little things—your dollies—you can grow a large quilt, or use the skills you have learned to grow your own design.

You could also make all the dolly quilts as a collection. There are loads of websites on the Net, showing off dolly quilt collections, both antique and modern. They look wonderful displayed on a wall, framed, or even made into a clutch of cushions to brighten up a couch.

Try to use the quilts in this book to find out more about growing your own quilting. Why do you choose the fabrics you do? Do your quilts look 'the same' every time, or is every one different? Do you usually choose the same style of fabrics for every quilt? Do you often make quilts with only three or four fabrics in them, or do you cram so many fabrics in that you can't see the wood for the trees? Do you love your quilts, do they make you happy—and why do you make them in the first place?

I make my quilts because if I didn't, I would be a very cranky girl indeed! I need to make them to feel happy and useful. They are something that is entirely mine but, at the same time, something that I share with others. All my life, I have had a creative outlet of some kind, but until I came to quilt designing, I didn't realise how unfulfilling those other outlets were to me. I love to make my quilts; I love to design them and

From little things— your dollies—you can grow a large quilt, or use the skills you have learned to grow your own design

to use them, and I love others to use them. Whether or not other people think they are good or worthy is to me a bonus—I would still make quilts even if no-one but my children saw them. They make me feel energised and excited and full of possibilities.

I design from my stash, and I encourage you to do the same. If you don't have a large stash, I encourage you to start growing one! You don't need huge amounts of fabric: even 20-centimetre pieces can be the seeds of a diverse quilt, somewhere down the line.

My stash is large, but it's never large enough. I don't ever feel bad about how much fabric I have—the fabric is as essential to my inspiration as the actual construction of the quilts.

Buy fabrics because you love them and because they make your heart sing, not because they have a specific purpose. One day, the perfect fabric will jump right into your hands from your cupboard, without your ever knowing the reason for which it was bought! These random discoveries are what make your fabric choices interesting and exciting rather than pre-determined.

Get excited, get passionate! Nothing is 'wrong' if you love the finished product. Go on, get growing—I mean, sewing.

Yes, I meant now! What are you waiting for?

Sarah Fielke

Choosing fabrics

*t*he question I am asked most often is how I choose my fabrics, and what makes me use certain fabrics together. I'm sorry to say that I don't have a definite answer for you. All I can do is tell you what kind of fabrics I buy and how I know that they are right together.

My stash is full of fabrics in different-sized graphics. This is just as important as having a good range of colours. My fabrics are divided by colour, but also often by tone and print size. I try to make sure that I have a good range of lights, mediums and darks in all the colours in my stash: for example, my blues range from a very pale powder blue through aqua and cerulean right through to a very dark navy. Within those colours, there will be small, medium and large prints, and always, always, spots and stripes.

I have lots of small graphics—little flowers, small checks and spots, tiny motifs and pin stripes. Reproduction ranges and shirtings and 1930s prints are great places to find smaller prints.

Then there are the medium-sized prints, the ones that would be the most present in most people's stashes. These prints include florals, tone-on-tones, stripes, checks and spots. Modern fabric ranges lean mainly into the medium range in both graphics and tone. That's all fine, but you need to make sure that you have variations in colour, graphic and tone if you want to create movement and interest in your quilts.

Many quilters shy away from large-scale prints, not knowing how to use them except in large pieces. I always have a good range of large prints in my stash—I love that when you cut a large print into small pieces, you get so much more diversity and interest into your quilt than you do with a smaller print, in conveniently co-ordinating colours! And, of course, a large print always makes a striking border.

There are three things I cannot live without. I have a huge stash of predominantly white fabrics that I love and hoard with a passion. They are indispensable when I make the kinds of quilts I love to make most. These fabrics have spots, stripes, floral prints, checks...but they are predominantly white. I also have a real passion for fabrics with little animals on them—I have literally hundreds and nearly all my quilts

You need to make sure that you have variations in colour, graphic and tone if you want to create movement and interest in your quilts

have an animal in them somewhere. And I never met a spot I didn't like! Spots are my neutrals—I use them as basics and backgrounds. A spot with an irregular spread becomes a neutral and recedes, whereas a regular print spot comes forward.

You will notice that I don't list solids as essential in my stash. That's because, as a rule, I don't use them. Even though, in this book, you will see a few quilts with 'plain' fabrics included in them, these fabrics are shot cottons or linens that have texture and layered colour rather than being a flat, solid fabric. I particularly like to use Kaffe Fassett's shot cottons, Oakshott fabrics and Essex linen.

OK, now you've planted the seeds of your stash, you want to know why I use fabrics together, and this is where it gets hard. Essentially, the answer is this.

When I start a new project, I go to the stash cupboard and pull out a few fabrics that I think would be a good start. Then I go through all my piles of fabric with those fabrics in mind. I don't have the original fabrics in sight, as the temptation then is to match everything up, and that takes all the surprise out of the colour combinations.

When I have a good pile of things that are making me smack my lips together, I put everything in one pile and start holding things up against each other. Sometimes, there are little piles 'brewing' all over the place in the studio, for days or weeks on end. The bonus of this is that sometimes when I clean up, things are put together that never were intended to go together, and then there's magic! The unexpected joy of two very different fabrics playing harmoniously together can be the highlight of my day. As a Gee's Bend quilter once said: 'Let chance be your creative director.'

When I am relatively happy with a pile (and often the original fabrics don't make the grade!), I start to cut pieces and put them on the design wall. I always work with a design wall so that I can stand back from pieces I have arranged, have a good long look and let them 'steep' a while longer. Sometimes, a piece I think is perfect looks totally different when it is cut up and on the wall.

Keep changing, keep moving things around. Try something different if you're not convinced. My fabric choice philosophy boils down to this—if it makes your heart sing, it's perfect.

As a Gee's Bend quilter once said: 'Let chance be your creative director.'

Before you begin...

Using this book

The quilts in this book are grouped into 10 pairs, with each pair consisting of a dolly quilt and a full-sized quilt that was inspired, in some way, by the dolly.

My suggestion would be—especially if you are a less experienced quilter—that you should make the dolly quilt before you attempt the larger version. The dolly quilts give you the opportunity to perfect a particular piecing technique or experiment with colours and fabrics before spending considerable time and money on a large project. Of course, you don't have to take my advice—you may want to get stuck right into the larger version without attempting the dolly. Or you may, indeed, plan to make only dolly-sized quilts and none of the large ones. It's entirely up to you, but whatever you choose to do, check out the basic information below before you begin and, when you get to the projects themselves, do take a few minutes to read through all the steps before you start.

Degree of difficulty

*

*

Straightforward piecing

**

More complex techniques

***

Complex techniques such as inset piecing

****

More than one complex technique required

A note on measurements

Measurements for patchwork and quilting are traditionally given in imperial units. This is still generally the case even in countries that have long used the metric system.

Many quilting accessories, such as rotary cutting mats and quilter's rulers, give measurements only in imperial. For the quilts in this book, imperial measurements are given in the cutting and sewing instructions, but fabric requirements are given in both metric and imperial.

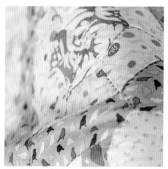
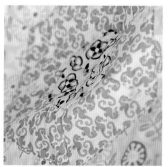

Fabrics and preparation

All fabric requirements listed under Materials and Tools are based on fabric that is 112 cm (44 inches) wide, unless specified otherwise. I recommend that all your fabrics be 100 per cent cotton or linen, and be ironed before cutting.

Many quilters prefer to wash, dry and iron cotton quilting fabrics before use, and this is an especially good idea with dark fabrics. Wash each fabric separately in warm water with a scrap of white cotton fabric to test if the colour runs. If it does, the fabric should be discarded or used for another purpose. Otherwise, when the quilt is washed, the colour may run and ruin the quilt.

Washing pre-shrinks fabric and removes all finishes added by the manufacturer. Such finishes can make the fabric stiffer and easier to sew; if you wish to restore the stiffness, spray the fabric lightly with spray starch before sewing.

Before sewing, remove the tightly woven edges (selvedges) from all fabrics. These shrink at a different rate from the rest of the fabric, so if they are left on and included in seams, they may cause the fabric to pucker and bunch when it is laundered.

Unless otherwise stated, all seam allowances are ¹/₄ inch throughout.

The dolly quilts give you the opportunity to perfect a particular piecing technique or experiment with colours and fabrics

Fat quarters

A 'fat quarter' is made by cutting one metre or one yard of fabric in half, first vertically, then horizontally. The resultant squarish piece, approximately 50 x 56 cm (in metric systems) or 18 x 22 inches (in imperial measurements), is sometimes a more useful size than a 'standard' quarter-metre or quarter-yard that is simply cut across the width of the fabric. Fat quarters are a good size for backing a dolly quilt.

General sewing and patchwork supplies

Rather than repeating this list under Materials and Tools for every project, I am assuming that you will have the following basic requirements before you begin:

- Sewing machine (unless you are a very patient hand-sewer!)
- $1/4$-inch sewing machine foot, for accurate sewing of seams
- Machine thread to match your chosen fabrics—see note on choosing threads, opposite
- Dress-making scissors—to be used only for cutting fabric
- Thread snippers, or small sharp scissors
- Scissors that can be used for cutting paper or template plastic
- Seam unpicker
- Pins
- Tape measure
- Quilter's ruler—it is handy to have two rulers of the same size to assist in cutting strips without having to turn the cutting mat around
- Rotary cutter—buy the best one you can afford
- Self-healing cutting mat
- Masking tape, for securing backing fabric to a flat surface and marking quilting lines
- Chalk pencil and gel pen, for marking quilting and appliqué lines
- Quilter's safety pins (if you are pinning quilt layers, rather than basting—see page 193)
- Quilter's hoop, for hand-quilting
- Quilter's thimble

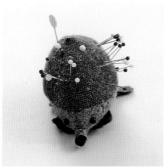

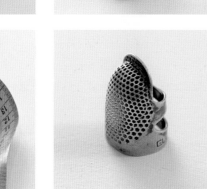
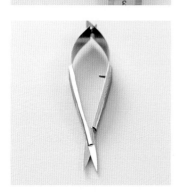

{note}

CHOOSING THREADS

Match the thread to the fabric when piecing: for example, when using cotton fabric, use cotton thread. Avoid using polyester thread with a cotton fabric; over time it will cut through the fibres of the cotton.

In most situations, cream, white or grey threads are appropriate for piecing. If using a multicoloured fabric, use a neutral thread, such as grey or beige, to match the tone of the background.

Using a design wall

If you're making a quilt that has a lot of blocks of different colours or tones, I really recommend laying them all out on a flat surface, such as the floor or a wall or, better still, on a design wall, made with batting or felt, which helps the cut shapes to stay in place. If you don't have space, you can even use a piece of flannel or an old sheet to lay your pieces out on to view, then fold it up and put it away when you are not working on the quilt.

By using a design wall, it is possible to 'audition' or sample colours or shapes before committing to sewing them together. You can move the blocks about until you get a pleasing arrangement, and check that the same fabrics aren't too close to each other, and that the eye is not drawn to particular blocks or areas at the expense of the rest of the design. Squinting at the quilt or looking at it through the lens of a camera can help you discern 'holes' or unbalanced areas. It is always a good idea to lay out the blocks and step back. However, if this isn't possible, cover a piece of cardboard with batting scraps and keep it next to the sewing machine. Lay out each block on the batting before sewing it together.

Special rulers

All of the quilts in this book can be made using a standard 24-inch quilter's ruler and the templates provided. However, occasionally I have included an optional specialised ruler in the Materials and Tools list. These rulers can make accurate cutting much quicker and easier, and if you wish to use them, then by all means do so. They are usually sold with detailed instructions for their use.

Half-square triangle ruler

A half-square ruler, also called a 45-degree triangle ruler, is useful, but not strictly necessary, for cutting half-square triangles. You can, of course, cut these triangles with your standard quilter's ruler by cross-cutting strips into squares, then cutting each square diagonally in half, giving two half-square triangles. (The size of the square that you cut when cutting half-square triangles in this way should always be $7/8$ inch larger than the desired finished size of the triangle.)

Specialised half-square triangle rulers, however, have already made allowance for the seam allowance at the point of the triangle, thus eliminating the 'ears' on the seam. This means that if you are using a

By using a design wall, it is possible to 'audition' or sample colours or shapes before committing to sewing them together

half-square triangle ruler, the size of your cut square should only be $1/2$ inch larger than the desired finished size of the triangle, not $7/8$ inch. The half-square triangles that you cut with this type of ruler will all have a blunt point.

Wedge ruler

Wedge rulers, also called circle segment, fan or Dresden plate rulers, are used for cutting accurate segments of a circle—or wedges—and come in a variety of brands and sizes. In this book, I have used an 18-degree wedge ruler to cut the wedges in *Hanging Lanterns*.

60-degree triangle ruler

This ruler is primarily used to cut equilateral triangles (each internal angle is 60 degrees and all three sides are the same length), but it is also useful for accurately cutting diamonds, half-diamonds and 30-degree triangles. I have used this ruler for *Peaks and Troughs* and *Stars in Your Eyes*.

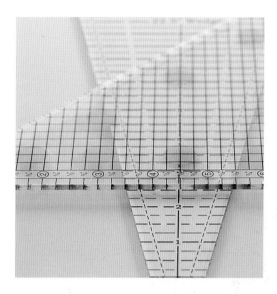

Specialised rulers can make accurate cutting much quicker and easier.

Finishing your quilt

Each of the projects takes you step-by-step through the construction of the quilt top. When you are ready to combine your completed top with the batting, backing and binding, turn to the Basics, layout and assembly section on page 182 for detailed instructions.

The projects

Row by row construction

Diamond Chips
Dolly quilt, 32 cm (12½ inches) square

Botanical Gardens
Throw, 189 cm (74½ inches) square

The secret to making both these quilts is simple—understanding that the blocks are constructed in rows of squares across the quilt, rather than in constructed blocks that are then sewn together, is the key. Practise by sewing together a smaller, more controlled number of squares and colours before you challenge yourself with the more complex colour layouts of *Botanical Gardens*. Using a design wall and a reducing glass or camera to check the placement and value of the fabrics in *Botanical Gardens* will make your job so much easier!

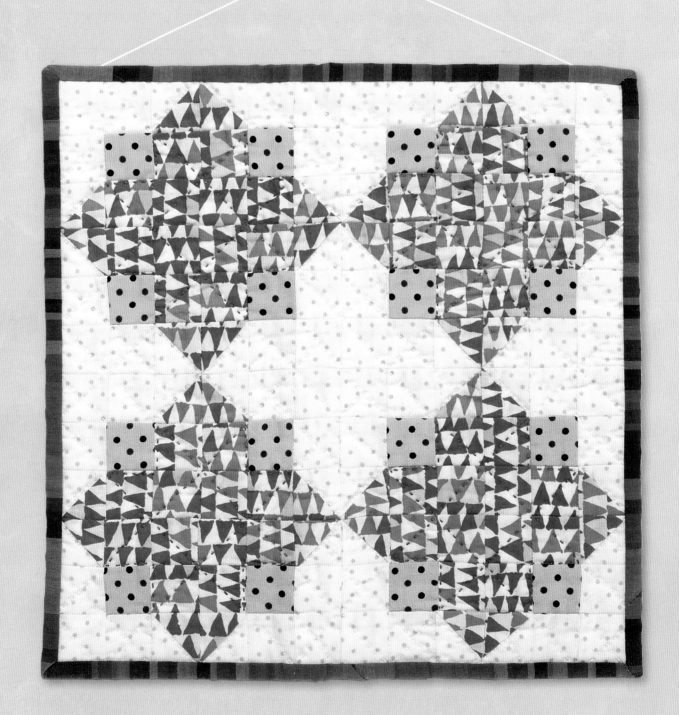

Diamond Chips

The blue and white fabrics in this quilt are what create the diamond sparkle in the pattern. The fabric used for the diamonds is a triangular graphic, which makes the diamond shape of the block seem more faceted.

Finished quilt size

Dolly quilt, 32 cm (12½ inches) square

Degree of difficulty

*

MATERIALS AND TOOLS

- 10 cm (4 inches) spotted white fabric
- 10 cm (4 inches) blue-patterned fabric with a strong graphic
- 10 cm (4 inches) spotted yellow fabric, or scrap
- 15 cm (6 inches) striped fabric for binding
- 1 fat quarter for backing
- 40 cm (16 inches) square cotton batting
- Half-square triangle ruler (optional, see page 24)
- White and blue perle cotton No 8 for quilting
- No 9 crewel embroidery needles for quilting
- General sewing and patchwork supplies (see page 22)

CUTTING

All fabrics are strip-cut across the width of the fabric from fold to selvedge unless otherwise specified or unless you are using a directional print.

FROM SPOTTED WHITE FABRIC, CUT:

- Two strips, 1½ inches wide. Cross-cut these strips to yield 48 squares, each 1½ inches.
- One strip, 1⅞ inches wide. Cross-cut this strip to yield 16 squares, each 1⅞ inches. Cross-cut these squares across one diagonal to yield 32 half-square triangles. Alternatively, cut your strip 1½ inches wide and use a half-square triangle ruler to cut these triangles.

FROM BLUE-PATTERNED FABRIC, CUT:

- Two strips, 1½ inches wide. Cross-cut these strips to yield 48 squares, each 1½ inches.
- One strip, 1⅞ inches wide. Cross-cut this strip to yield 16 squares, each 1⅞ inches. Cross-cut these squares on one diagonal to yield 32 half-square triangles. Alternatively, cut your strip 1½ inches wide and use a half-square triangle ruler to cut these triangles.

FROM SPOTTED YELLOW FABRIC, CUT:
- One strip, 1½ inches wide. Cross-cut to yield 16 squares, each 1½ inches.

FROM STRIPED BINDING FABRIC, CUT:
- Two strips, 3 inches wide. Set aside for binding.

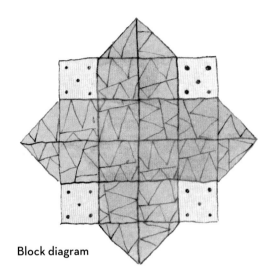

Block diagram

Constructing the quilt top

1 Begin laying out the pieces for each block according to the Block diagram and the photograph of the quilt. The quilt is put together in rows (rather than in complete blocks), so lay out all of the squares in their rows until the whole quilt is spread in front of you on a table or a piece of batting. Your quilt should be 12 squares across each row and 12 rows down.

2 Sew the first row together into a strip. When you reach the half-square triangles, sew the triangles together into a square across the diagonal (Diagram 1). Press the seam towards the darker fabric, trim the 'ears', and then sew the square to the strip, and continue. Press all the seams towards the dark fabrics.

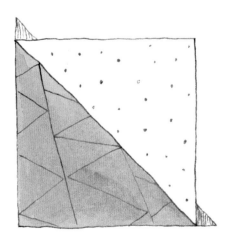

Diagram 1

3 Sew the second row. Press the seams towards the dark fabrics.

4 Continue until you have completed 12 rows. Now sew the first row to the second row, being careful to match the seams when the squares meet. Continue until you have sewn 12 rows together. Press the top carefully and make sure it is square. Your quilt top is complete.

Backing, quilting and binding

Using masking tape, tape the backing fabric, face down, onto a table, smoothing out any creases as you go. Lay the batting piece onto the backing, and then the quilt top on top. Smooth any creases and hand-baste the three layers together using large stitches and working from the centre out. As this is only a small quilt, it does not need a lot of basting. The backing and batting should be larger than the top for ease of quilting; don't be tempted to trim them back.

Refer to pages 190–199 for instructions on finishing.

{note on quilting}

I hand-quilted *Diamond Chips* using white perle cotton No 8 in a criss-cross fashion over the whole quilt, except the yellow squares. Where the grid crosses the blue-patterned squares, I changed to blue cotton thread.

Botanical Gardens

Flowers bloom and leaves sway in the lush botanical gardens of this quilt. Large–scale floral prints and co–ordinating graphics are the secret to making your own Botanical Garden bloom. Be sure to include a wide variety of prints, but make certain that the pairs of fabrics you choose are complementing each other, not contrasting, and you will create a blended garden bed just like the one shown here.

Finished quilt size
Throw, 189 cm (74½ inches) square

Degree of difficulty
*

MATERIALS AND TOOLS

- 10 cm (4 inches) each of 8 different light-blue and 8 different dark-blue fabrics

- 10 cm (4 inches) each of 8 different light-green and 8 different dark-green fabrics

- 10 cm (4 inches) each of 8 different light-orange or light-yellow and 8 different dark-orange or dark-yellow fabrics

- 10 cm (4 inches) each of 8 different light-pink or light-red and 8 different dark-pink or dark-red fabrics

- 50 cm (20 inches) dark-brown fabric for accent squares

- 10 cm (4 inches) medium floral fabric for border inserts

- 90 cm (1 yard) large floral fabric for border

- 70 cm (27 inches) striped fabric for binding

- 4.2 m (4⅝ yards) backing fabric

- 210 cm (83 inches) square cotton batting

- General sewing and patchwork supplies (see page 22)

CUTTING

All fabrics are strip-cut across the width of the fabric from fold to selvedge unless otherwise specified or unless you are using a directional print.

FROM EACH OF THE 10-CM (4-INCH) PIECES OF LIGHT AND DARK FABRICS, CUT:

- One strip, 3⅞ inches wide, across the width of the fabric, giving a total of 64 strips. Separate the fabrics into 32 pairs, each containing a light and a dark strip from the same colourway (eight pairs of each colourway).

FROM EACH COLOURWAY PAIR, CUT:

- Two pairs of squares, each 3⅞ inches (four squares in total). Cross-cut these pairs of squares on one diagonal into four pairs of half-square triangles (eight half-square triangles in total). Trim the remaining section of each colourway pair to be 3½ inches wide.

FROM EACH TRIMMED PAIR, CUT:

- Six pairs of squares, each 3½ inches (12 squares in total). Set the eight half-square triangles and 12 squares from each colourway pair aside in their pairs (zip-lock bags are handy here for keeping things in order) and continue with the remaining fabric pairs until you have cut all the squares and triangles for 32 pairs.

FROM DARK-BROWN FABRIC, CUT:

- Five strips, 3½ inches wide. Cross-cut these strips into 3½-inch squares—you will need 49 squares in all.

FROM BORDER INSERT FABRIC, CUT:

- One strip, 3½ inches wide. From this strip, cross-cut seven pieces, each 6 x 3½ inches.

FROM BORDER FLORAL, CUT:

- Six strips, 6 inches wide.

FROM RED BINDING FABRIC, CUT:

- Nine strips, 3 inches wide. Set aside for binding.

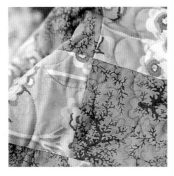

{note}

I recommend using a design wall for this quilt. You can also use a half-square triangle ruler to cut your triangles, if you prefer (see page 24).

Constructing the quilt top

1 Using the photograph of the finished quilt and the Block diagram, begin by laying out the pieces for each row. Your quilt should be 21 squares across each row and 21 rows down.

Each 'block' of the quilt contains the four pairs of half-triangles and the six pairs of squares that you cut from a light/dark colourway pair, as well as four brown accent squares. However, the quilt top is constructed square by square, and row by row, rather than a block at a time. As you lay out the rows, you will see how the blocks in each colourway are formed and it helps to visualise the design in terms of blocks.

(Using a design wall is a great way to lay out your pieces, as you can see your colours clearly. Follow the layout of alternating colours as in the picture, but don't be too worried about where each fabric goes yet. It is much better to lay the fabric down, and then move the colours around until you are happy with the layout.)

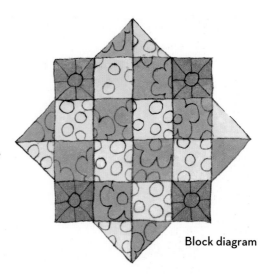

Block diagram

2 You will also see from the photograph that the edges of the patchworked quilt top are composed of half-blocks and, in the upper left- and lower right-hand corners, of quarter-blocks. For these rows, you will need to divide some of your sets of square and triangle pairs into the appropriate number.

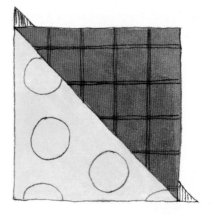

Diagram 1

3 When you are happy with the arrangement of your squares, sew the first row together into a strip. When you come to the half-square triangles, sew the triangles together into a square (Diagram 1). Press the seam allowance towards the darker fabric, trim off the 'ears' at each corner and then sew the completed square to the strip, and continue. Press all the seams towards the dark fabrics.

4 Sew the second row. Press the seams towards the dark fabrics.

5 Continue in this way until you have completed all 21 rows of the quilt top. Now sew the first row to the second row, being careful to match the seams when the squares meet. Continue until you have sewn all 21 rows together. Press the top carefully and make sure it is square.

Border

6 Beginning and ending with a 6-inch border insert piece, sew the seven inset pieces and six floral border strips together, end to end, into one long strip.

7 Measure your quilt through the centre in both directions to get the true width. It should measure 63½ inches. (If it does not, you should adjust the following border measurements.)

8 Cut two strips from the assembled border fabric, each 63½ inches long. Find the centre of one edge of the quilt and the centre of one border strip and pin, then pin the ends together. Pin in between, easing if needed. Sew and repeat with the opposite border. Press.

9 Measure the quilt across the middle again with the borders attached. Cut the remaining two borders to this measurement. Attach the remaining two borders as above. Your quilt top is complete.

Backing, quilting and binding

Cut the backing fabric in half crosswise, giving two pieces, each 210 cm (83 inches) long. Trim the selvedges and sew the pieces together along the length to form one backing piece. Press the seam allowance open.

Refer to pages 190–199 for instructions on finishing.

{note on quilting}

I had *Botanical Gardens* machine-quilted by Kim Bradley in an all-over floral pattern.

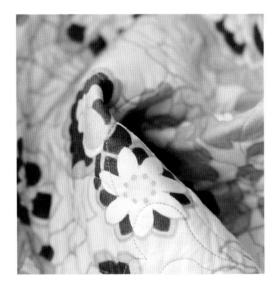

Strip piecing

Rebel with a Rotary
Dolly quilt, 40.5 cm (16 inches) square

Sandwich Short of a Picnic
King single, 152 x 222 cm (60 x 87½ inches)

Both these quilts are strip-pieced. Strip piecing is a way to create your own 'fabric' from which to cut another shape. In both of these quilts, triangles are cut from strips sewn together into meterage, to create striped triangles.

There are so many applications of this technique. Try out the dolly quilt or *Picnic* quilt to get your eye in, and then try making other shapes—diamonds, rectangles, squares. You can even strip piece and cut circles to appliqué. Just be sure to sew onto a cloth or paper foundation if you are going to have too many bias edges!

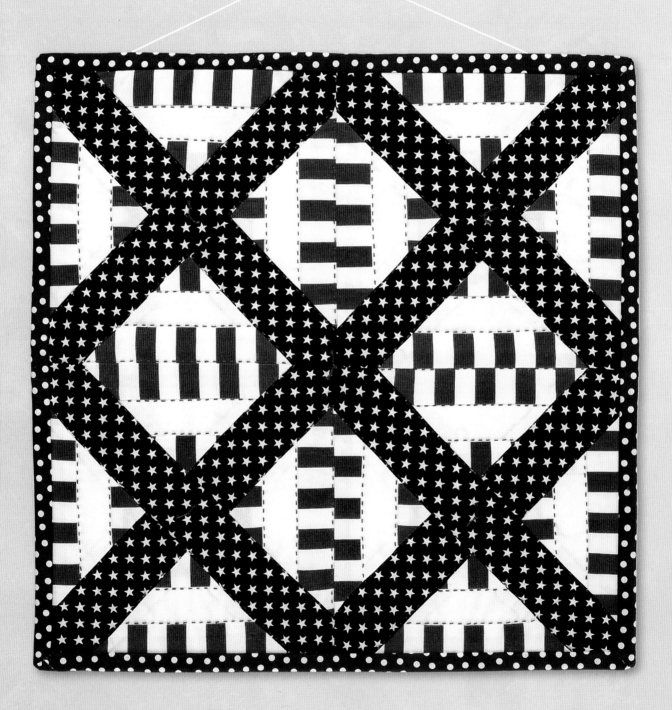

Rebel with a Rotary

Unintentionally, this little quilt came out looking like the rebel flag! In red, white and blue though, it could be an Australian flag, an English flag, an American flag, a French flag—why not make it in red, white and green for Italy? Or dive into your stash and create your own flag of the Patchwork Nation.

Finished quilt size

Dolly quilt, 40.5 cm (16 inches) square

Degree of difficulty

*

MATERIALS AND TOOLS

- 15 cm (6 inches) red-and-white striped fabric

- 10 cm (4 inches) white fabric

- 15 cm (6 inches) dark-blue star fabric

- 15 cm (6 inches) dark-blue fabric for binding

- 1 fat quarter for backing

- 50 cm (20 inches) square cotton batting

- 2B pencil

- Template plastic

- Red perle cotton No 8 for hand-quilting and tying

- No 9 crewel embroidery needles for quilting

- General sewing and patchwork supplies (see page 22)

TEMPLATES

Trace the Template A triangle (on pattern sheet) onto template plastic with a sharp 2B pencil and cut out accurately using sharp scissors (but not your fabric scissors).

CUTTING

All fabrics are strip-cut across the width of the fabric from fold to selvedge unless otherwise specified or unless you are using a directional print.

FROM RED-AND-WHITE STRIPED FABRIC, CUT:
- Four strips, 1½ inches wide.

FROM WHITE FABRIC, CUT:
- Two strips, 1½ inches wide.

FROM DARK-BLUE STAR FABRIC, CUT:
- Three strips, 2 inches wide. Cross-cut these strips to yield eight strips, each 2 x 5½ inches, and four strips, each 2 x 12½ inches.

FROM BINDING FABRIC, CUT:
- Two strips, 3 inches wide. Set aside for binding.

Constructing the quilt top

1 Sew together two sets of three strips, each set consisting of two red-and-white striped strips with a white strip in between (Diagram 1). Press the seams towards the striped fabric.

2 Using Template A, cut 16 triangles in total from the two pieced strips. Alternatively, using the 45-degree angle on your patchwork ruler, cut a 45-degree bias line from your strip set. Re-align the ruler and cut a 45-degree angle at the top of the strip. Cut 16 triangles in total (Diagram 2).

3 Following Diagram 3, join one shorter side of a triangle to one edge of a 5½ x 2-inch star fabric strip. Sew a second triangle to the other edge of the strip to form a half-block. Make sure to line up the end of the strip with the 90-degree corner of the triangles so that the other end sticks out for trimming later. Repeat with all eight pairs of triangles to make eight half-blocks in total.

4 Sew two half-blocks together with a 12½-inch star strip in between. To do this, fold the star strip in half and finger-press the centre crease. Do the same with the triangle strip and match the creases before sewing, so that the strip is sticking out the same amount at each end for trimming later. Make four blocks in this way.

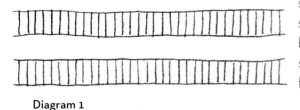

Diagram 1

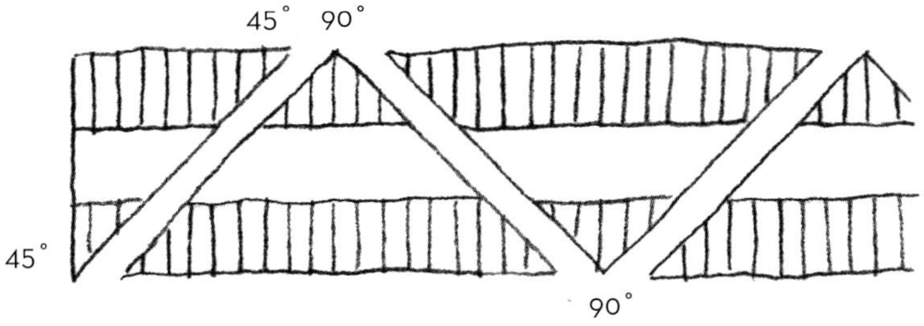

45˚ 90˚

45˚

90˚

Diagram 2

5 Using your patchwork ruler, trim the blocks to measure 8¼ inches square (Diagram 4).

6 Sew two pairs of blocks together, taking care to match the seams on the diagonals. Now, sew the pairs together across the middle seam of the quilt. Press. Your quilt top is complete.

Backing, quilting and binding

Using masking tape, tape the backing fabric, face down, onto a table, smoothing out any creases as you go. Lay the batting piece onto the backing, and then the quilt top on top. Smooth any creases and hand-baste the three layers together using large stitches and working from the centre out. As this is only a small quilt, it does not need a lot of basting. The backing and batting should be larger than the top for ease of quilting; don't be tempted to trim them back.

Refer to pages 190–199 for instructions on finishing.

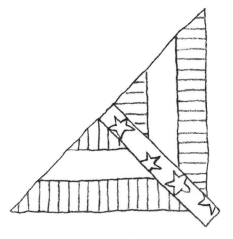

Diagram 3

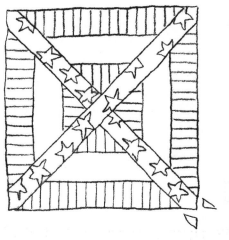

Diagram 4

{note on quilting}

I hand-quilted *Rebel with a Rotary* using red perle cotton No 8 along the 'down' sides of the strip-pieced seams and around the outside of each square. I also tied a knot of perle cotton in the centre of the Xs made by the star fabric.

Sandwich Short of a Picnic

There's a beautiful memory behind this simple quilt. When I was a tiny little girl, about two or three years old, I would go to my grandma's house for the day, so my mum could have a break and look after my baby brother. We did all sorts of different things together, but my favourite thing was rowing our boats.

Grandma would announce that it was 'a nice day to row our boats to Bobbin Head', and we would go straight to the kitchen and spend the morning making ribbon sandwiches and baking a sultana slice for the journey. I was allowed to help with everything but the knives.

At lunchtime, we would collect my grandpa from the study with his hat and his pipe, and head out to the picnic blanket on the front lawn and eat our picnic.

After lunch, my marvellous grandma would get out two battered cardboard boxes, we would both climb into one—with grandma's floral skirts hitched up around her knees—and proceed to row our 'boats' and have an adventure.

This quilt is about my trips to Bobbin Head with my grandma and her beautiful ribbon sandwiches.

Finished quilt size
King single, 152 x 222 cm (60 x 87½ inches)

MATERIALS AND TOOLS

- 15 cm (6 inches) each of eight different fabrics for outer sandwich fillings (see Note page 55)

- 10 cm (4 inches) each of eight different fabrics for inner sandwich fillings

- 1 m (1⅛ yards) plain white fabric for bread

- 2.5 m (2¾ yards) 'picnic blanket' fabric for triangles and binding

- 70 cm (27 inches) green checked fabric for binding

- 5 m (5½ yards) backing fabric

- 180 x 230 cm (72 x 90 inches) cotton batting

- General sewing and patchwork supplies (see page 22)

CUTTING

All fabrics are strip-cut across the width of the fabric from fold to selvedge unless otherwise specified or unless you are using a directional print.

FROM EACH OF THE EIGHT DIFFERENT OUTER SANDWICH FILLINGS FABRICS, CUT:
- Two strips, 2½ inches wide (16 strips in total).

FROM EACH OF THE EIGHT DIFFERENT INNER SANDWICH FILLINGS FABRICS, CUT:
- One strip, 2½ inches wide (8 strips in total).

FROM WHITE FABRIC, CUT:
- 16 strips, 2½ inches wide.

FROM THE PICNIC BLANKET FABRIC, CUT:
- Three strips, 21 inches wide. Cross-cut these strips into six squares, each 21 inches. Cross-cut these squares on both diagonals to yield four quarter-square triangles from each square, for a total of 24 quarter-square triangles. (You will actually only need 22.)
- Three strips, 10½ inches wide. Cross-cut these strips into six squares, each 10½ inches. Cross-cut these squares on one diagonal to give 12 half-square triangles. (You will actually only need 10.)

FROM THE GREEN CHECKED FABRIC, CUT:
- Nine strips, 3 inches wide. Set aside for binding.

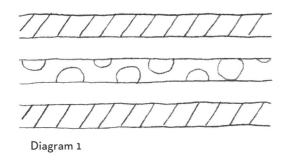

Diagram 1

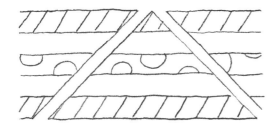

Diagram 2

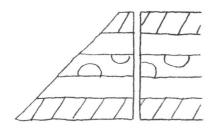

Diagram 3

Constructing the quilt top

Making the sandwiches

1 To make your sandwiches, sew together eight sets of 'fillings' and 'bread' along the length of the strips (Diagram 1). Each 5-strip set should read:

- Outer filling strip
- Bread strip
- Inner filling strip
- Bread strip
- Outer filling strip

(I realise that sandwiches usually have the bread on the outside not the fillings, but the fillings are brighter and provide more contrast! You will have to use your imagination.) When you have sewn a 5-strip set together, press the seams away from the white bread fabric.

2 Using the 45-degree angle on your patchwork ruler, cut a 45-degree bias line across your strip set. Re-align the ruler and cut at a 45-degree angle from the top of the strip, giving a triangle. (The internal angle at the top of this triangle will be 90 degrees, as shown.) Cut three triangles from each of the eight fabric sets (Diagram 2)—24 triangles in total.

3 From the remaining piece at the end of each strip set, cut one half-square triangle. Using the 45-degree angle already cut in the strip, measure along ¾ inch from the top of the angle and cut down at a 90-degree angle (Diagram 3)—eight half-triangles in total.

Piecing the rows

4 Using a design wall or a bed for colour balancing, lay the sandwich blocks and 'picnic rug' triangles out according to the photograph of the quilt. Move the sandwich blocks around until you are happy with their positions. Refer to the photograph for placement of the half-square triangles.

5 Beginning with the top row, sew the triangles together in rows across the quilt. Make sure to clip the 'ears' off the triangles, and then press the seams towards the sandwiches.

6 When you have pieced all the rows, join the rows together down the quilt. An easy way to make sure that the points meet is to insert a pin through the point of both seam allowances as you sew, and remove it just as you sew up to it. Make sure that the needle goes right into the place when the pin was (Diagram 4). Press. Your quilt top is complete.

Backing, quilting and binding

Cut the backing fabric crosswise in half into two pieces, each 250 cm (99 inches) long. Remove the selvedges and stitch the pieces together up the long sides. Press the seam allowance open and press the backing piece carefully.

Refer to pages 190–199 for instructions on finishing.

Refer to pages 190–199 for instructions on finishing.

{*note*}

If you are intending your triangles to represent the sandwiches in the picnic, as mine do, think about your fillings before you choose the colours. My fillings include some of my grandma's favourites, such as tuna and celery, cheese and tomato, and chicken and asparagus. You could also use wholemeal or multi-grain bread if you like! My grandma always used soft white 'bunny bread' with the crusts cut off, so that's what I have used here.

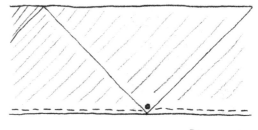

Diagram 4

{*note on quilting*}

I had *Sandwich Short of a Picnic* machine-quilted by Kim Bradley in a pattern of butterflies, using white thread.

Deconstructed piecing

The Woodpile
Dolly quilt, 29 x 27 cm (11½ x 10½ inches)

Dandelions
King single, 150 x 211 cm (59 x 83 inches)

Wonky piecing can be daunting if you have never attempted it before. The concept of cutting pieces without a ruler when every patchwork pattern has urged you to be so careful can be scary! To master this technique, you need to let go of your worries about points that meet and straight seams, and do what feels right. Everything can be trimmed straight when the block is finished and then everything goes together smoothly.

I recommend trying out the technique on *The Woodpile* dolly before launching into the *Dandelion* quilt—there are a lot of little flowers in there!

The Woodpile

These little wonky log cabin blocks are sure to whet your appetite for deconstructed piecing. I decided they wouldn't really be log cabins and had to be woodpiles—whoever lived in those wonky little cabins would be banging their head on the roof much too often!

Degree of difficulty **

Finished quilt size

Dolly quilt, 29 x 27 cm (11½ x 10½ inches)

MATERIALS AND TOOLS

- Scrap fabrics of different blues, greens, pinks, purples and oranges, cut roughly into strips, at least 1½ inches wide x 5 inches long

- 10 cm (4 inches) dark-brown fabric for border triangles

- 10 cm (4 inches) pink-patterned fabric for border triangles

- 15 cm (6 inches) multicoloured striped fabric for binding

- 1 fat quarter for backing

- 30 cm (12 inches) square cotton batting

- Purple and green silk or cotton for hand-quilting

- Quilting needles ('betweens')

- General sewing and patchwork supplies (see page 22)

CUTTING

Do not use a ruler to cut your scrap pieces if you can help it—you don't want the seams to be straight or the block will look too symmetrical.

FROM SCRAP FABRICS, CUT:

- Rough strips, approximately 1½ inches wide—do not use a ruler to cut these.

FROM DARK-BROWN FABRIC, CUT:

- Two strips, 1½ inches wide. Cross-cut these strips into 38 squares, each 1½ inches.

FROM PINK-PATTERNED FABRIC, CUT:

- Two strips, roughly 1½ inches wide.

FROM BINDING FABRIC, CUT:

- Two strips, 3 inches wide. Set aside for binding.

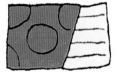

Diagram 1

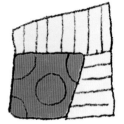

Diagram 2

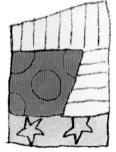

Diagram 3

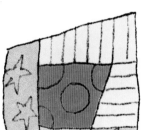

Diagram 4

Constructing the quilt top

1 Begin by cutting a small piece for the centre of each block. Decide what colour the 'logs' are going to be. Each block has two colourways for the logs, one for each side. If the block is blue and green, for instance, I have used a different colour for the centre. Sew a strip of one colour to the side of the centre piece and trim off the end of the strip (Diagram 1). Finger-press the seam open. It is fine to angle the fabrics on top of each other so that the seams are not straight.

2 Sew a strip of the same colour to the next side of the centre block, trim and finger-press the seam open (Diagram 2).

3 Sew a strip of the second colour to the next side of the block (Diagram 3).

4 Complete a round of logs by sewing another strip of the second colour to the last side of the centre block and trim (Diagram 4).

5 Keep sewing around the block in this manner until the block is at least 5 inches square. Take the block to the ironing board, press all the seams flat, and then trim the block to be 5 x 4½ inches.

6 Repeat to make four blocks: two that are predominantly blue and green and two that are pink and yellow, or purple and orange.

7 Arrange the blocks according to the photograph, or in an order that pleases you. Sew two blocks together along the 5-inch side to make a pair, and repeat with the other two blocks. Sew the blocks together to form the quilt centre. Press.

Pink/brown border

8 Take a brown square and lay the pink strip over the top of it at an angle, right sides together (Diagram 5). This angle is not critical—in fact each of your finished squares will be slightly different. Sew, and then trim the brown fabric away from the seam allowance. Press and trim the piece to 1½ inches square (Diagram 6). Repeat to make 38 squares.

9 Sew the squares together into two strips of eight squares and two strips of 11 squares, with all the pink diagonals pointing in the same direction (see the photograph of the quilt for guidance).

10 Sew the two strips of eight squares to the top and bottom of the quilt, and the two strips of 11 squares to either side. Press. Your quilt top is complete.

Backing, quilting and binding

Using masking tape, tape the backing fabric, face down, onto a table, smoothing out any creases as you go. Lay the batting piece onto the backing, and then the quilt top on top. Smooth any creases and hand-baste the three layers together using large stitches and working from the centre out. As this is only a small quilt, it does not need a lot of basting. The backing and batting should be larger than the top for ease of quilting; don't be tempted to trim them back.

Refer to pages 190–199 for instructions on finishing.

Diagram 5

Diagram 6

{note on quilting}

I hand-quilted *The Woodpile* using silk thread, quilting along the logs in one side of the block, ⅛ inch apart, and in the ditch on the other side of the logs.

Dandelions

I wandered lonely as a cloud,
That floats on high o'er vales and hills
When all at once I saw a crowd
A host of...
(from the poem 'Daffodils' by William Wordsworth)

OK, well they're not golden daffodils, they're white dandelions, but I think these fluffy little flowers remind me of my childhood more than any other flower. Our local park certainly had a host of them, and we used to pick them and blow all the seeds away into the park gardens to make fairy wishes. I'm sure the gardeners didn't love us much. Our blowing must have been creating dandelions faster than they could pull them out. You can make your own childhood fairy wishes with this quilt, or piece all the flowers in different colours for a field of wildflowers instead.

Finished quilt size

King single, 150 x 211 cm (59 x 83 inches)

Degree of difficulty **

MATERIALS AND TOOLS

- 60 cm (24 inches) each of seven different plain green fabrics for the background

- 10 cm (4 inches) each of eight different yellow fabrics for the daisy centres

- White or pale print fabrics (or scraps), totalling about 2.6 m (2⅞ yards), for dandelion petals

- 65 cm (26 inches) lime-green fabric for setting triangles and corners

- 70 cm (28 inches) spotted yellow fabric for binding

- 4.6 m (5 yards) backing fabric

- 180 x 230 cm (71 x 91 inches) cotton batting

- General sewing and patchwork supplies (see page 22)

CUTTING

All fabrics are strip-cut across the width of the fabric from fold to selvedge unless otherwise specified or unless you are using a directional print.

FROM EACH OF THE SEVEN GREEN FABRICS, CUT:

- Nine strips, 2½ inches wide. Cross-cut these nine strips into 142 squares (in total), each 2½ inches. There will be a few extra. From the seven fabrics, you need a total of 992 green 2½-inch squares.

FROM EACH OF THE EIGHT YELLOW FABRICS, CUT:

- One strip, 2½ inches wide. Cross-cut each strip into 16 squares, each 2½ inches. From the eight fabrics, you need a total of 124 yellow 2½-inch squares. (There will be a few extra.)

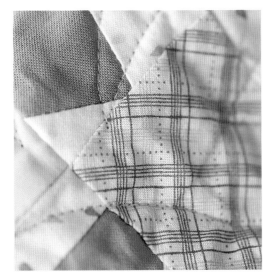

FROM THE WHITE FABRICS, CUT:

- Strips of any length, 2½ inches wide. If you are using fabric lengths, cut all of your fabrics up into 2½-inch strips. If using scraps, make sure that your pieces are at least 2½ inches square.

FROM LIME-GREEN FABRIC, CUT:

- Two strips, 10¼ inches wide. Cross-cut these strips into eight squares, each 10¼ inches. Cross-cut these squares on both diagonals to yield 32 quarter-square triangles for the setting triangles (you only need 30). From the remaining piece of fabric, cut two squares, each 5⅞ inches, and cross-cut on one diagonal to yield two half-square triangles for the corners.

FROM SPOTTED YELLOW BINDING FABRIC, CUT:

- Nine strips, 3 inches wide. Set aside for binding.

Constructing the quilt top

Making a dandelion 'star'

1 Each dandelion star begins with eight random green squares and one yellow square (Diagram 1). Take four of these green squares to be the background of the petals.

Diagram 1

2 From your 2½-inch wide strips of white fabric, cut a strip that is longer than the angle you are going to sew. Lay the white strip over one of the four green squares, right sides together, overlapping the pieces at odd angles. Remembering to allow for seams in your angle, sew the white strip onto the green square (Diagram 2). Trim the excess green away from the seam, as shown. Fold the white fabric over and press flat (Diagram 3). Trim the edges of the white strip to be square with the original green fabric square—that is, 2½ inches square (Diagram 4).

Diagram 2

{tip}

For a quick method of sewing the star-point squares, see Diagram 9 on page 67.

3 Using a scrap of the same white fabric, repeat Step 2 on the other side of the green square, being sure to use a different angle for the petal point (Diagram 5). Trim, as before, into a 2½-inch square (Diagram 6).

Diagram 3

Diagram 4

4 Repeat Steps 2 and 3 with the three remaining green squares. This makes the units for one complete dandelion.

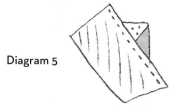

Diagram 5

Diagram 6

5 Sew the dandelion squares into rows and then sew the rows together (Diagram 7). You have now completed one dandelion.

6 Repeat the process until you have 124 dandelions, mixing the greens and whites well as you go (noting, however, that each individual flower is made from a single white fabric). Press the blocks.

Diagram 7

Assembling the blocks

7 Using a design wall or a bed for colour balancing, lay the dandelion blocks out in 10 rows of seven blocks on point. There will be nine rows of six blocks on point in between. Move the blocks around until you are happy with their positions.

8 Beginning at one corner, sew the blocks together in diagonal rows across the quilt, beginning and ending each row with a setting triangle (Diagram 8). Please note that the setting triangles are too large for the blocks of the quilt. This is so that when you have finished sewing the top together, you can trim the triangles and ensure that the quilt is square.

9 When you have sewn all the rows of blocks, sew the rows together in strips, matching the seams as you go, until you have sewn all the rows together. Press. Your quilt top is complete.

Backing, quilting and binding

Cut the backing fabric in half crosswise, giving two pieces, each 230 cm (90 inches) long. Trim the selvedges and sew the pieces together along the length to form one backing piece. Press the seam allowance open.

Refer to pages 190–199 for instructions on finishing.

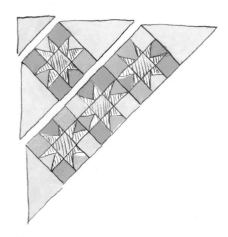

Diagram 8

Diagram 9: Quick method for star-point squares

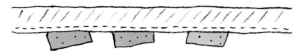

a. sew to strip

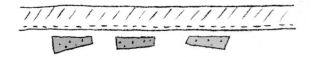

b. trim excess

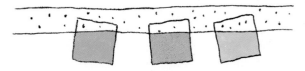

c. trim cut squares

{note on quilting}

I had *Dandelions* machine-quilted by Kim Bradley in a swirling pattern, using green thread.

Appliqué with bias strips

Spring
Dolly quilt, 53 x 51 cm (21 x 20 inches)

Whirligig
Throw, 161 cm (63½ inches) square

The techniques here are simple but excellent ones to add to your patchwork arsenal. If you have never tried my method of needle-turn appliqué before, *Spring* is a great place to do it. I use this method because I find it quick and easy, while still allowing me to achieve accurate shapes and placement.

Making and shaping bias vines for quilts can be a tedious job, but using pre-made bias tape or a bias maker can give you great results in half the time.

You will find that the placement of the leaves in both quilts is a rather fluid thing. Having the leaves placed irregularly on both quilts adds to the whimsical feel.

Spring

'Spring has sprung, the grass is riz...' This joyful dolly quilt would make an excellent cushion to brighten up a dark corner.

Finished quilt size
Dolly quilt, 53 x 51 cm (21 x 20 inches)

Degree of difficulty ******

MATERIALS AND TOOLS

- 1 deep-purple fat quarter for background
- Wide variety of scraps for leaves and butterfly
- 1.5 m (1²⁄₃ yards) x 12 mm-wide (½ inch) pre-made spotted green bias tape
- 25 cm (10 inches) fabric for binding
- 60 cm (24 inches) backing fabric
- 60 cm (24 inches) square cotton batting
- Cotton threads to match appliqué fabrics
- 2B pencil
- Template plastic
- Appliqué glue
- Straw needles for appliqué

- Silver gel pen
- Perle cotton No 8 in orange and grey for hand-quilting (optional)
- No 9 crewel embroidery needles for quilting
- General sewing and patchwork supplies (see page 22)

TEMPLATES
Trace Leaf and Butterfly templates (on pattern sheet) onto template plastic with a sharp 2B pencil and cut out accurately using sharp scissors (but not your fabric scissors).

CUTTING
All fabrics are strip-cut across the width of the fabric from fold to selvedge unless otherwise specified or unless you are using a directional print.

FROM THE DEEP-PURPLE FAT QUARTER, CUT:
- One piece, 20 x 21 inches, for background.

Constructing the quilt top

Appliqué

Read the instructions for Appliqué on page 186 before proceeding.

1 Place the plastic Leaf template onto the right side of one of the scrap fabrics and trace around it using the gel pen. Using small, sharp scissors, cut the shape out, a scant ¼ inch outside the gel pen line.

2 Repeat this process with the other appliqué scraps until you have cut 39 Leaves and one Butterfly shape.

3 Fold the purple background square into quarters to find the centre and finger-press the crease. Fold again on the diagonals and finger-press the crease. Using the photograph as a guide, take the gel pen and draw a large, widely spaced spiral onto the background, starting at the centre point of the square and radiating out.

4 Take the square to the ironing board and place one end of the green bias tape onto the beginning of the gel line, in the centre of the piece. Working slowly, iron the bias tape along the gel line, stretching it around the curves until you have pressed the tape into the shape of your spiral.

5 Lift the edges of the tape, put a drop of appliqué glue onto the back and press it down. It will take a few moments to dry.

6 Using the photograph as a guide, glue the leaves into place around the vine in a spiral. Take care not to glue too close to the edge of the fabric. If the spirals of your vine are too close together in some places to fit a leaf, don't worry—just overlap the leaves onto the next spiral. Glue the butterfly in the centre of the quilt.

7 When the glue is dry and the shapes are fused to the background, begin by sewing on the spiral vine. Start in the centre of the quilt, on the inside curve. Sew all the way along the inside of the vine until you reach the other end, then go back to the middle and sew around the outside of the vine. Sewing in the same direction will prevent puckering.

8 Next, sew the leaves and butterfly. Thread a straw needle with cotton to match the fabric you are appliquéing. Finger-press along the silver gel line all around the edge of the shape, turn the edge under along the pressed line and sew the shape to the background, using small stitches. You will need to clip into the inside curves to turn them under. Press. Your quilt top is complete.

Backing, quilting and binding

Using masking tape, tape the backing fabric, face down, onto a table, smoothing out any creases as you go. Lay the batting piece onto the backing, and then the quilt top on top. Smooth any creases and hand-baste the three layers together using large stitches and working from the centre out. As this is only a small quilt, it does not need a lot of basting. The backing and batting should be larger than the top for ease of quilting; don't be tempted to trim them back.

Refer to pages 190–199 for instructions on finishing.

{note on quilting}

I hand-quilted *Spring* using orange perle cotton No 8. I outline-quilted all the leaves and the vine, using orange, then outline-quilted around the butterfly in grey and, finally, quilted the butterfly's antennae.

Whirligig

I think that I enjoyed making this quilt the most of any in this book. I love to hand-appliqué, and the combination of the bright scraps and Anna Maria Horner's beautiful rose print in the large triangles made hand-quilting a joy. The added dimension of the free tabs in the outer border gives the quilt a fluttery feeling that complements the windmill of flowers in the centre.

Finished quilt size

Throw, 161 cm (63½ inches) square

Degree of difficulty
**

MATERIALS AND TOOLS

- 1.7 m (1⅞ yards) yellow-and-blue-spotted fabric for Medallion and Outer Border

- 1.6 m (1¾ yards) blue floral fabric for Setting Triangles

- 1 m (1⅛ yards) spotted blue fabric for Narrow Borders and binding

- 1 pink fat quarter for Pollen

- 20 cm (8 inches) spotted brown fabric for Flowers

- 4 m (4⅜ yards) x 12 mm-wide (½ inch) spotted green bias tape for vines

- Wide variety of scraps for Leaves and Border Tabs (you will need about 1.7 m (1⅞ yards) fabric in total; scraps need to be at least 8 cm (3 inches) wide)

- 3.8 m (4⅛ yards) backing fabric

- 188 cm (74 inches) square cotton batting

- Cotton threads to match appliqué fabrics

- 2B pencil

- Template plastic

- Appliqué glue

- Straw needles for appliqué

- Silver gel pen

- Perle cotton No 8 in blue and yellow for hand-quilting

- No 9 crewel embroidery needles for quilting

- General sewing and patchwork supplies (see page 22)

TEMPLATES

Trace Leaf, Flower and Pollen templates (on pattern sheet) onto template plastic with a sharp 2B pencil and cut out accurately using sharp scissors (but not your fabric scissors).

CUTTING

All fabrics are strip-cut across the width of the fabric from fold to selvedge unless otherwise specified or unless you are using a directional print.

FROM YELLOW-AND-BLUE SPOTTED FABRIC, CUT:

- One square, 41 inches, for Centre Medallion.
- Seven strips, $3\frac{1}{2}$ inches wide, for Outer Border.

FROM BLUE FLORAL FABRIC, CUT:

- Two squares, each 30 inches. Cross-cut these squares on one diagonal to yield a total of 4 half-square triangles for the Setting Triangles.

FROM SPOTTED BLUE FABRIC, CUT:

- 11 strips, $1\frac{1}{2}$ inches wide, for inner and outer Narrow Borders.
- Seven strips, 3 inches wide, for binding.

FROM ASSORTED SCRAPS, CUT:

- 240 squares, each 3 inches, for the Border Tabs.

Constructing the quilt top

Appliqué

Read the instructions for Appliqué on page 186 before proceeding.

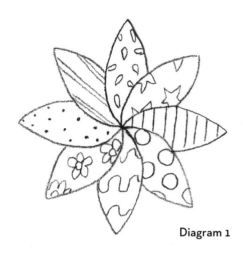

Diagram 1

1 Place the Flower template onto the right side of the spotted brown fabric and trace around it using the gel pen. Using small, sharp scissors, cut the shape out, a scant ¼ inch outside the gel pen line. Repeat to cut a total of eight Flowers.

2 Repeat this process with the other appliqué templates. Cut eight Pollen shapes from the pink fabric and a total of 112 Leaves from scrap fabric.

3 Fold the Medallion square into quarters to find the centre and finger-press the creases. Fold again on the diagonals and finger-press the creases. Using the photograph as a guide, cut and arrange the bias tape vines onto the background until you are happy with the placement. They should begin near the centre of the medallion, run up along the creases and then curve over as they reach the top. Remember that your medallion square is cut two inches too large and will be trimmed back after completing the appliqué, so don't take the vines right to the edge.

4 Lift the edges of the vines and put a drop of glue onto the fabrics and press them down. Take care not to glue too close to the edge of the fabric. You only need a small spot of glue to make the pieces stick. They will take a few moments to dry.

5 Glue a brown-spotted Flower to the end of each vine and a Pollen shape above each Flower. Following Diagram 1, glue eight Leaves onto the background in a spiral flower pattern for the centre of the quilt.

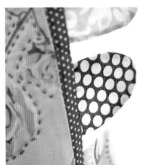

6 When the glue is dry and the shapes are fused to the background, select a shape on which to begin sewing. Thread a straw needle with cotton to match the fabric you are appliquéing. Finger-press along the silver line all around the edge of the shape, turn the edge under along the pressed line and sew the shape to the background, using small stitches. You will need to clip into the inside curves to turn them under. The bias will not need turning under, as it already has a folded edge. When you sew the centre flower, turn under each petal edge until you get to where it is overlapped by the next one.

7 When you have appliquéd these shapes, arrange the Leaves along the vines in six pairs of Leaves along each stem, and one Leaf in the 'v' shape where the vines meet the central flower. These leaves are not supposed to be perfectly symmetrical—place them in a way that is pleasing to your eye and not measured. Glue in place and stitch.

8 When you have completed the appliqué, trim the Medallion square to be 39 inches.

Narrow inner borders

9 Trim two of the spotted blue 1½-inch strips to 39 inches long. Find the centre of one strip and the centre of the quilt top and pin. Pin the ends, then pin in between, easing as you go if needed. Sew. Repeat with the opposite side of the square.

10 Trim two more spotted blue strips to 41 inches long. Repeat Step 9 and sew the borders to the remaining sides of the quilt top. Press the seams towards the Centre Medallion.

Diagram 2

Diagram 3

Diagram 4

Setting triangles

11 Find the centre of one side of the quilt and the centre of the diagonal side of one blue floral setting triangle and pin. Pin the ends, then pin in between and ease. Sew. Repeat with the opposite side of the quilt.

12 Sew the two remaining triangles to the remaining sides of the quilt, as above. Trim the quilt top to be square, trimming the triangles to a ¼-inch seam above the point of the centre square on point. Press the seams towards the blue triangles.

Narrow outer borders

13 Sew the remaining seven spotted blue 1½-inch strips together, end to end, into one long strip. Measure the quilt through the centre. Cut a piece from the strip to this measurement. Pin and sew the blue strip to one side of the quilt, as for Step 9, and then sew another border to the opposite side in the same way.

14 Measure the quilt through the centre in the opposite direction and cut and sew border strips, as before. Press the seams towards the blue triangles.

Border tabs

15 Place the 3-inch scrap squares together in random pairs, right sides facing each other. Randomly cut a tab-shaped piece with a curved end at one end and a straight end at the other (Diagram 2). Sew from the straight end along the edge and around the curve, leaving the straight end open (Diagram 3). Clip along the curves, turn the Tab right side out and press flat (Diagram 4). Make approximately 120 tabs of different sizes and shapes.

16 Arrange approximately 30 Tabs along one side of the quilt, right sides together, with the curved edge of the Tabs facing inwards and the straight edges level with the edge of the quilt. Pin into place. Depending on the width of your Tabs, you may want more or fewer than 30 to achieve a look you like.

17 Sew the Tabs to the quilt ¼ inch from the edge of the quilt. Repeat for the remaining three sides.

Outer border

18 Sew all the 3½-inch yellow-and-blue-spotted Outer Border strips together, end to end, into one strip.

19 Measure your quilt through the centre in both directions to get the true width. Cut two Outer Border strips to be the measurement of the quilt in one direction. Find the centre of a side of the quilt top and the centre of one of the Outer Borders. Pin the centres together, then pin the ends. Pin in between, easing if needed. Sew, catching the edges of the tabs as you go. Repeat with the opposite border. Press.

20 Measure the quilt across the centre again, from Outer Border to Outer Border. Cut the remaining two Outer Borders to this measurement and attach them as for Step 19. Press the border towards the centre of the quilt, carefully pressing the tabs flat to the border. Your quilt top is complete.

Backing, quilting and binding

Cut the backing fabric crosswise in half into two 190 cm (74 inches) long pieces. Remove the selvedges and stitch the pieces together up the long seams. Press the seam allowance open and press the backing piece carefully.

Refer to pages 190–199 for instructions on finishing.

{note on quilting}

I hand-quilted *Whirligig* using blue and yellow perle cotton No 8. I outline-quilted all the appliqué, using blue, and cross-hatched the Medallion background and the Outer Border in a 1½-inch grid, using yellow. I then outline-quilted the flowers in the blue setting triangles, using blue cotton. Finally, I outline-quilted each of the Tabs in blue.

Flying geese and foundation piecing

Geese Around the World
Dolly quilt, 34 cm (13½ inches) square

North by North East
Queen size, 231 cm (91 inches) square

A Flying Geese block is not hard to make after you have made one or two accurately, so I have given you two different techniques with these two quilts: traditional Flying Geese in *North By North East* and foundation piecing for *Geese Around the World*.

The trick to foundation piecing is to take care with how large you cut your fabric pieces. Be sure to be generous when cutting, so that you can overlap the paper foundations with room to spare, and you won't find yourself unpicking all your hard work.

Both quilts use bright triangles and white contrast to effect, and both create their own flying patterns.

Geese Around the World

The geese here are flying in a circle, creating a whirling pattern. If you try this and like foundation piecing, this pattern would make a wonderful bed-sized quilt.

Finished quilt size

Dolly quilt, 34 cm (13½ inches) square

Degree of difficulty **

MATERIALS AND TOOLS

- 16 scraps, at least 6 x 3½ inches, or 3½ inches of 8 pink, orange and green fabrics for 'geese'

- 35 cm (14 inches) white fabric for background

- 15 cm (6 inches) checked fabric for binding

- 1 fat quarter for backing

- 50 cm (20 inches) square cotton batting

- 4 sheets of foundation paper, or any thin A4 paper

- Aqua perle cotton No 8 for quilting

- No 9 crewel embroidery needles for quilting

- General sewing and patchwork supplies (page 22)

TEMPLATES

Trace or photocopy the foundation pieces for Templates A, B, C and D (on pattern sheet) onto A4 paper. You need four copies of each template to make the circle of geese. Roughly cut out the templates from the paper, NOT on the ¼-inch seam allowance line, but outside it.

CUTTING

All fabrics are strip-cut across the width of the fabric from fold to selvedge unless otherwise specified or unless you are using a directional print.

FROM THE COLOURED SCRAP FABRICS, CUT:
- 16 pieces, about 3½ x 6 inches, for the 'geese'.

FROM WHITE FABRIC, CUT:
- Four strips, 3½ inches wide.

FROM CHECKED FABRIC, CUT:
- Two strips, 3 inches wide, for the binding.

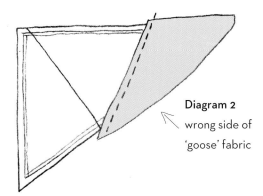

Diagram 1
wrong side of
white fabric

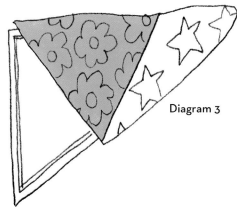

Diagram 2
wrong side of
'goose' fabric

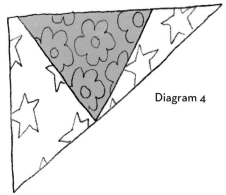

Diagram 3

Diagram 4

Constructing the quilt top

Foundation piecing

Read the instructions for Foundation piecing on page 184 before proceeding.

1 Begin sewing with a Template A piece. Place a white background piece and a coloured goose piece right sides together with white background uppermost and place the foundation paper on top (Diagram 1). The white piece should be positioned so that it covers piece 1 on the template. Check to make sure that the coloured piece will also cover piece 2 when the seam is opened after sewing.

2 Adjust the stitch length on your sewing machine to be quite small, about 1.8 or 2, depending on the make of your machine. Position the fabrics so that they are approximately ¼ inch out from the sewing line and sew along the line on the paper. Trim away any excess fabric ¼ inch from the seam line (Diagram 2).

3 Turn the paper over and iron the fabric open (Diagram 3). Cut another piece of white background fabric to fit piece 3. Position the white fabric, right sides together, against the goose fabric. Check that it will cover Piece 3 when it is open, then turn to the paper side and stitch along the sewing line. Turn to the fabric side and press the fabric open.

4 Turn the piece over to the paper side again and trim the shape along the outer ¼-inch line using a rotary cutter (Diagram 4). Set aside without removing the paper, and repeat with all the other template shapes, alternating the patterned fabrics as you go so that they are well mixed.

Constructing the blocks

5 When you have pieced together all the foundation shapes take one each of Template A, B, C and D. Lay them out in order (Diagram 5).

6 Take Template A and Template B and put a pin through the corners of the ¼-inch seam to line them up. Make sure the pieces are well matched. Sew along the seam line on the paper side. Repeat to join Template C and Template D to the row of geese, forming a square.

7 Make four squares in this way and press all the seams away from the geese points.

8 When you have completed four squares, remove the paper backing by carefully tearing it away from the seams. Use tweezers or a pin to get any small pieces out that are stuck in the stitches.

Joining the blocks

9 Referring to the photograph for placement, lay the four squares out so that the geese form a circle. Stitch the top two squares together into a pair and repeat with the bottom two. Join the pairs, taking care to match the centre seam. Press. Your quilt top is complete.

Backing, quilting and binding

Using masking tape, tape the backing fabric, face down, onto a table, smoothing out any creases as you go. Lay the batting piece onto the backing, and then the quilt top on top. Smooth any creases and hand-baste the three layers together using large stitches and working from the centre out. The backing and batting should be larger than the top for ease of quilting; don't be tempted to trim them back.

Refer to pages 190–199 for instructions on finishing.

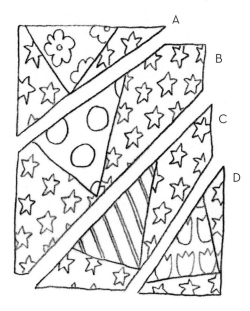

Diagram 5

{note on quilting}

I hand-quilted Geese *Around the World* using using aqua perle cotton No 8, quilting along the down side of all the foundation seams on the white fabric.

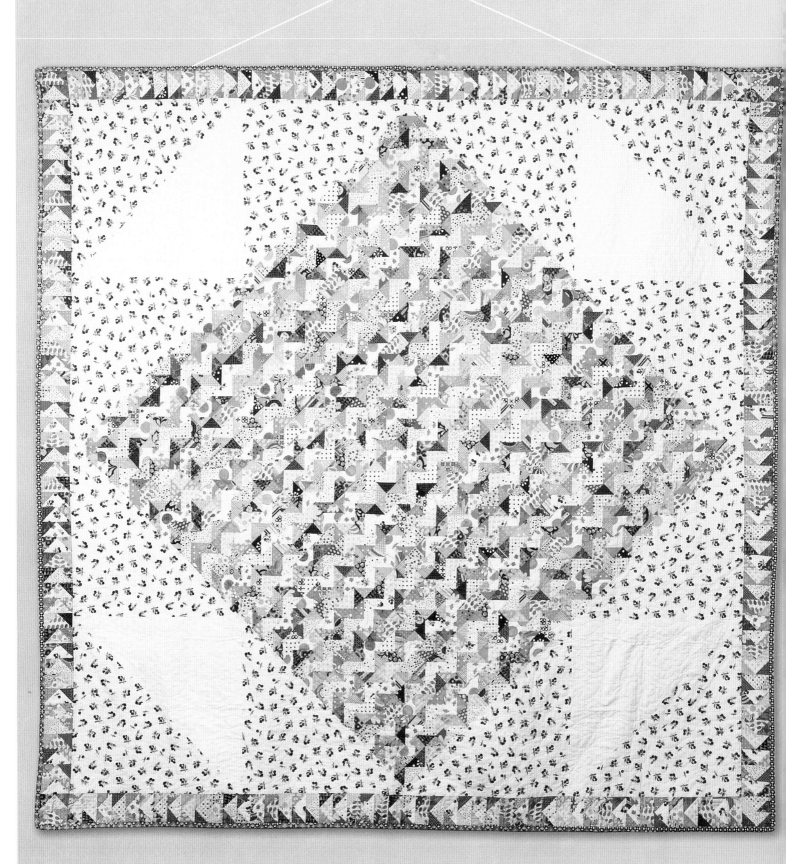

North by North East

All those geese, flying south for the winter! Or here in the southern hemisphere, flying north. Or perhaps they are flying north after winter, and coming home to all those spring colours. Whatever you decide, these geese will fly into an amazing formation to form the centre of this quilt.

Finished quilt size

Queen size, 231 cm (91 inches) square

Degree of difficulty **

MATERIALS AND TOOLS

- 50 cm (20 inches) each of 10 different prints with white backgrounds

- 5.1 m (5⅝ yards) in total of a wide range of different coloured prints, or 30 cm (12 inches) each of 15 different prints

- 3.75 m (4⅛ yards) cherry-print fabric for setting triangles

- 1.3 m (1½ yards) tone-on-tone white fabric for setting triangles

- 75 cm (30 inches) green fabric for binding

- 7.5 m (8⅓ yards) backing fabric

- 2.5 m (98 inches) square cotton batting

- General sewing and patchwork supplies (page 22)

CUTTING

All fabrics are strip-cut across the width of the fabric from fold to selvedge unless otherwise specified or unless you are using a directional print.

FROM EACH OF THE 10 WHITE BACKGROUND FABRICS, CUT:

- Seven strips, 2¼ inches wide. Cross-cut these strips into rectangles, 4 x 2¼ inches, yielding a total of 696 pieces.

FROM ONLY ONE OF THE WHITE BACKGROUND FABRICS, CUT:

- One strip, 2⅝ inches wide. Cross-cut this strip into 16 squares, each 2⅝ inches. Cut these squares in half along one diagonal to yield 32 half-square triangles. (You could also cut a total of 16 squares from scraps of several white fabrics, rather than just one, if you prefer.)

FROM THE COLOURED FABRICS, CUT:

- Enough strips, 2¼ inches wide, to cross-cut into a total (from all the fabrics) of 1,392 squares.

- Enough strips, 2⅝ inches wide, to cross-cut into 16 squares (in total). Cut these squares in half along one diagonal to yield 32 half-square triangles.

FROM THE CHERRY-PRINT FABRIC, CUT:
- Six squares, each 23 inches. Cut these squares in half on one diagonal to yield 12 half-square triangles.

FROM TONE-ON-TONE WHITE FABRIC, CUT:
- Two squares, each 23 inches. Cut these squares in half on one diagonal to yield four half-square triangles.

FROM GREEN BINDING FABRIC, CUT:
- Ten strips, 3 inches wide. Set aside for binding.

Constructing the quilt top

Flying geese panel

1 Matching the corners, lay a coloured 2¼-inch square on one end of a white rectangle, right sides together, and sew diagonally across the square (Diagram 1).

2 Trim the seam allowance (Diagram 2) and press the triangle open. Repeat with another square of a different fabric on the other end of the white rectangle (Diagram 3). Trim the seam allowance again. Press open (Diagram 4). This is one Flying Geese unit.

3 Repeat Steps 1 and 2 to make 696 Flying Geese units.

4 Join a white half-square triangle and a coloured half-square triangle together along the diagonal edge and press open. Trim the 'ears' from the triangles to make a square unit. Make 32.

{note}

I recommend using a design wall for this quilt (see page 24).

Diagram 1

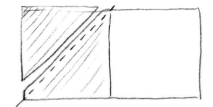

Diagram 2

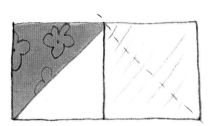

Diagram 3

Diagram 4

Quilting from little things...

5 On the design wall, lay out your Flying Geese in rows, as follows, mixing the colours well. Row A begins and ends with a square unit. There are 15 Flying Geese units in this row and the point of the white triangle should point downwards. Row B consists entirely of Flying Geese units (no squares). There are 16 Flying Geese in this row and the points on the white triangles should point upwards. Starting with a Row A and alternating with a Row B, lay out 32 rows, referring to the photograph for guidance. Move the Geese around within the rows until you are happy with the colour placement, taking care to keep the orientation of the white triangle points correct.

6 Sew the Geese together into their rows until you have pieced 32 rows.

7 Join the rows, beginning at the top of the panel and working down. Take care to match the ends together and pin each point carefully. Press the panel.

Setting triangles

8 Referring to the photograph of the quilt for placement, join a cherry print triangle to either side of a white solid triangle and press the seams towards the cherry fabric. Join a cherry triangle to the remaining side of the white triangle (Diagram 5). Make four of these units for the corners of the quilt.

9 Find the centre of the long edge of the corner unit and the centre of one side of the centre panel and pin. Sew the corner unit to the quilt, matching the centres.

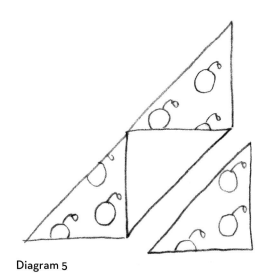

Diagram 5

{note}

The setting triangles are too large for the centre panel, but they will be trimmed back.

10 Next, sew a corner unit in the same manner to the opposite corner of the quilt.

11 Join the other two corners to the quilt top in the same way and press.

12 Measuring through the centre in both directions, trim the quilt to 84½ inches square.

Border

13 Take the remaining 200 Flying Geese units and, mixing the colours well, sew them together along their long edge into two strips of 48 geese and two strips of 52 geese.

14 Find the centre of the top edge of the quilt and the centre of a strip of 48 geese and pin. Pin the ends and pin in between, easing if needed. Sew and repeat with the bottom edge of the quilt. Press the seams towards the setting triangles.

15 Attach the longer borders to the sides of the quilt in the same manner. Press. Your quilt top is complete.

Backing, quilting and binding

Cut the backing fabric crosswise into three pieces, each 250 cm (100 inches) long. Trim the selvedges and sew the pieces together along the length to form one backing piece. Press the seam allowance open.

Refer to pages 190–199 for instructions on finishing.

{note on quilting}

I had *North by North East* machine-quilted by Kim Bradley in an all-over floral pattern.

Inset piecing

Peaks and Troughs
Dolly quilt, 48 x 54 cm (18³/₄ x 21¹/₄ inches)

Stars in Your Eyes
King single, 164 x 208 cm (64¹/₂ x 82 inches)

Inset piecing is the technique of setting a piece of fabric into an L- or Y-shaped seam. It doesn't have to be as mysterious as it sounds—careful marking of the ¹/₄-inch point and accurate sewing will get you there. Practising on the *Peaks and Troughs* dolly is also very helpful, before tackling the more difficult seams of *Stars in Your Eyes.*

Peaks and Troughs

Diamonds go up and diamonds go down, forming the zigzags
in this quilt. Enlarging this quilt to a single or double bed size
with zigzags all the way across would be spectacular.

Finished quilt size

Dolly quilt, 48 x 54 cm (18¾ x 21¼ inches)

Degree of difficulty ***

MATERIALS AND TOOLS

- 5 cm (2 inches) each of
  9 different blue-and-green
  fabrics, or scrap

- 25 cm (10 inches) natural linen
  for background

- 15 cm (6 inches) blue striped
  fabric for binding

- 56 x 64 cm (22 x 25 inches)
  backing fabric

- 55 x 61 cm (22 x 25 inches)
  cotton batting

- Variegated blue perle cotton
  No 8 for hand-quilting

- No 9 crewel embroidery needles,
  for quilting

- 60-degree triangle ruler
  (optional, see page 29)

- Template plastic and 2B pencil
  (optional)

- General sewing and patchwork
  supplies (see page 22)

TEMPLATES

If you are not using the 60-degree triangle ruler,
trace Templates A, B, C and D (on pattern sheet)
onto template plastic with a sharp 2B pencil. Cut
out accurately using sharp scissors.

CUTTING

All fabrics are strip-cut across the width of the
fabric from fold to selvedge unless otherwise
specified or unless you are using a directional print.

FROM EACH OF THE NINE BLUE-AND-GREEN FABRICS, CUT:

- One strip, 1½ inches wide.

FROM THE LINEN, CUT:

- One strip, 3½ inches wide. Using the 60-degree
  ruler or Templates A, B and D, cross-cut this
  strip into five 60-degree diamonds with 4-inch
  sides (Template A), two half-square triangles
  (Template B) and two 60-degree triangles
  (Template D).

- One strip, 2½ inches wide. Using the 60-degree
  ruler or Template C, cut five half-diamonds from
  this strip, with 8¾-inch bottom edges. (Note that
  these triangles are slightly too large, but the extra
  can be trimmed back when piecing.)

• Two strips, 2 inches wide, for the Outer Border.

FROM THE BLUE STRIPED FABRIC, CUT:
• Two strips, 3 inches wide. Set aside for binding.

Constructing the quilt top

Diamonds

1 Take a set of three blue/green strips. Sew them together along the length of the strip in the order you have chosen until you have a piece of patchwork that is 3½ inches wide x the width of the fabric (Diagram 1). Press all the seams to one side.

2 Repeat Step 1 until you have made three pieces like this.

3 Using the 60-degree ruler or Template A, from each patchwork strip cut six diamonds with 4-inch long sides (Diagram 2). You need to cut 18 diamonds in all.

4 Using the photograph as a guide, lay the quilt out, taking care that the strips of fabrics in the diamonds lie in alternating positions to form the pattern.

5 Begin by piecing together Row 1 of the pieced diamonds in their zigzag pattern. Begin and end each seam ¼ inch from the end of each seam so that you can set the other pieces into the Y-shaped space of the blocks.

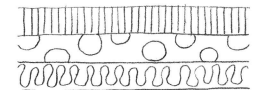

Diagram 1

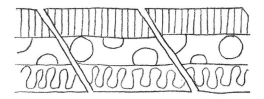

Diagram 2

Diagram 3

Row 1

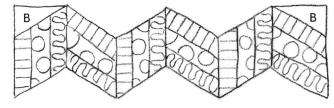

6 Sew a Template B linen half-square triangle to either end of the strip as shown (Diagram 3). Press all the seams towards the pieced diamonds.

7 Next, piece a Template C linen half-diamond into the Y seam. (Because the C triangles are too large, you should match the inner points first and allow the excess to extend beyond the outer edge.) Begin sewing at the outer end of the seam and sew the pieces together until you are ¼ inch from the trough of the Y at the inner point. When you reach this point, leave your needle in the fabric, lift the presser foot, pivot the fabric on the needle and lower the presser foot again. Continue sewing to the end of the next seam, first making sure that the fabrics are lying flat (Diagram 4).

8 Piece in the next Template C linen half-diamond in the same way, followed by the second Template B linen half-square triangle. Trim the upper edge square, remembering to leave ¼-inch seam allowance.

9 Next, piece a Template A linen diamond into the Y seam of the first and third pair of pieced diamonds (Diagram 5).

10 Sew together Row 2 of the pieced diamonds. Piece a linen diamond into the middle Y seam of this row, and then join the two rows together (Diagram 6).

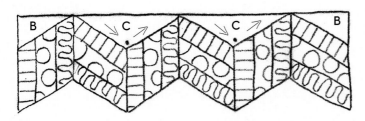

Diagram 4

Row 1

Pivot at the

Y seam

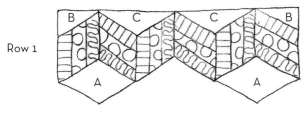

Row 1

Diagram 5

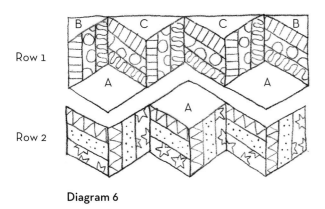

Row 1

Row 2

Diagram 6

Row 1

Row 2

D

A

Diagram 7

11 Sew a Template D linen 60-degree triangle to the first diamond piece and a linen diamond into the second Y seam of Row 2 (Diagram 7).

12 Piece together Row 3 of diamonds and sew a linen diamond A into the first Y seam, and a Template D triangle onto the last diamond. Join this row to the quilt top (Diagram 8).

13 Inset-piece three Template C linen half-diamonds into the last three Y seams (Diagram 9), noting again, that the Template C triangles are too large—see Step 7, above. Press, trim the excess seam allowance and check that your quilt is square.

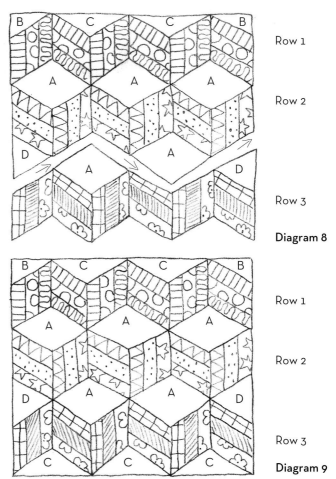

Row 1

Row 2

Row 3

Diagram 8

Row 1

Row 2

Row 3

Diagram 9

Quilting from little things...

Border

14 Sew the two border strips together into one long strip. Measure your quilt through the centre across the shorter measurement to get the width. Cut two border strips to this measurement.

15 Find the centre of a short side of the quilt top and the centre of one of the borders. Pin the centres together, pin the ends, then pin in between, easing if needed. Sew and repeat with the other short border. Press.

16 Now measure the quilt through the middle along the longer measurement. Cut and attach the long borders, as before. Press. Your quilt top is complete.

Backing, quilting and binding

Using masking tape, tape the backing fabric, face down, onto a table, smoothing out any creases as you go. Lay the batting piece onto the backing, and then the quilt top on top. Smooth any creases and hand-baste the three layers together using large stitches and working from the centre out. As this is only a small quilt, it does not need a lot of basting. The backing and batting should be larger than the top for ease of quilting; don't be tempted to trim them back.

Refer to pages 190–199 for instructions on finishing.

{note on quilting}

I hand-quilted *Peaks and Troughs* by outlining the diagonal lines in the diamonds using variegated perle cotton No 8. I also quilted along the down side of the seams in the pieced diamonds.

Stars in Your Eyes

All your favourite fabrics can sparkle and pop in this quilt. Pick your bright and happy colours to spark against the white fabric, add a wonderful large floral border and this is a recipe for success. You could also use a black background fabric and make this a fantastic boys' quilt.

Degree of difficulty ***

Finished quilt size
King single, 161 x 208 cm (63½ x 82 inches)

MATERIALS AND TOOLS

- 1.1 m (1¼ yards) aqua-and-white spotted fabric for setting diamonds

- 15 cm (6 inches) each of 6 sets of 5 fabrics for stars, or 60 strips of scrap at least 2½ inches wide (fabrics should be bright and in a range of different colours and patterns)

- 30 cm (12 inches) deep-pink fabric for Inner Border

- 1.7 m (1⅞ yards) cream-and-pink floral for Outer Border

- 60 cm (24 inches) multicoloured striped fabric for binding

- 3.6 m (4 yards) backing fabric

- 180 x 225 cm (70 x 88 inches) cotton batting

- Perle cotton No 8 in aqua, deep pink, candy pink, lime green and orange for hand quilting

- 1-inch wide masking tape for marking quilting lines

- No 9 crewel embroidery needles for quilting

- 60-degree triangle ruler (optional, see page 29)

- General sewing and patchwork supplies (see page 22)

TEMPLATE

If you are not using the 60-degree triangle ruler, trace Template A (on pattern sheet), onto template plastic with a sharp 2B pencil. Cut out accurately using sharp scissors.

CUTTING

All fabrics are strip-cut across the width of the fabric from fold to selvedge unless otherwise specified or unless you are using a directional print.

FROM AQUA-AND-WHITE SPOTTED FABRIC, CUT:

- Seven strips, 5³⁄₈ inches wide. From these strips, cut 42 diamonds with a 6¹⁄₄-inch long side, using the 60-degree line on your patchwork ruler or the 60-degree triangle ruler. For greater accuracy, you can use Template A as a guide.
- One strip, 3¹⁄₈ inches wide, for the half-diamonds. Using the 60-degree line on your ruler and Template A as a guide, cut four half-diamonds from the strip.

FROM EACH OF THE STAR FABRICS, CUT:

- Two strips, 2¹⁄₂ inches wide. You should have a total of 60 strips. Separate these strips into 12 sets of five fabrics, co-ordinating the colours as you go.

FROM DEEP-PINK FABRIC, CUT:

- Seven strips, 1¹⁄₂ inches wide. Set aside for Inner Border.

FROM CREAM-AND-PINK FLORAL FABRIC, CUT:

- Eight strips, 8¹⁄₂ inches wide. Set aside for Outer Border.

FROM MULTICOLOURED STRIPED FABRIC, CUT:

- Eight strips, 3 inches wide. Set aside for binding.

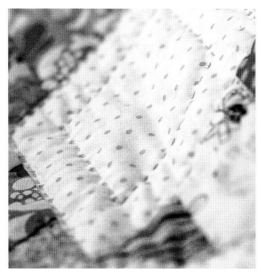

{*note*}

I recommend using a design wall for balancing the colours in this quilt (see page 24).

Constructing the quilt top

Stars (make 11 + two half-stars)

1 Take a set of five fabrics. Sew them together along the length of the strip in the order you have chosen, until you have a piece of patchwork that is 10½ inches wide x the width of the fabric. Press all the seams to one side (Diagram 1). Repeat with the remaining sets of fabrics until you have 12 patchworked strips.

2 Iron a pieced strip in half along the length, wrong sides together (Diagram 2). Take care not to distort the strips as you press.

3 Using the 60-degree ruler or Template A, cut six diamonds from each strip by placing the wide end of the ruler (or template) along the fold of the fabric and the squared-off tip at the raw edge (Diagram 3). Cut along the edges on each side, moving the ruler along the strip until you have cut six diamonds. When the diamonds are opened out, they should look like the one in Diagram 4.

4 From the remaining fabric in some of the strips, use the triangle template to cut six half-diamonds for the edges and four quarter-diamonds for the corners of the top. (Remember to allow for ¼-inch seam allowance on the straight edges of these half- and quarter-diamonds.)

5 When you have cut all the pieced diamonds, take the six diamonds from one set and piece three of them together to form a half-star (Diagram 5). Begin piecing ¼ inch in from the 'corner' join to make setting the background diamonds easier. Take care to press the seams in opposite directions to make a neat join. Make a matching half-star in the same way.

6 Join the two half-stars together across the centre to form a star, again leaving ¼ inch open at the corners (Diagram 6). Press.

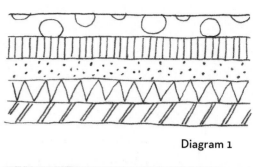

Diagram 1

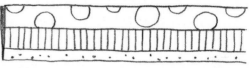

Diagram 2

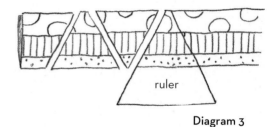

ruler

Diagram 3

{tip}

If you have cut carefully, the remaining scrap triangles from each strip can be pieced together to make a beautiful border, or into hexagons to use in another project.

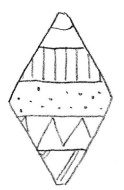

Diagram 4

Diagram 5

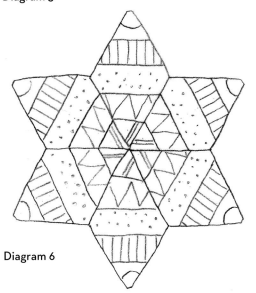

Diagram 6

7 Repeat Steps 5 and 6 until you have made 11 full stars and 2 half-stars.

Background diamonds

8 Lay the stars out on a design wall (or the floor) and balance the colours until you are happy with their arrangement. This is also a good way to keep track of the piecing together of the rows, which can be confusing if you don't have everything in front of you.

9 You can see from the Assembly diagram, that only one star is pieced into a complete hexagon, while the others are constructed in a different order. To inset-piece the diamonds on the whole hexagon star, begin at the outside point of the star and sew in to the inner corner of the star. Leave the needle in the fabric when you get ¼ inch from the corner. Raise the presser foot and pivot the diamond around on the needle so that it lies flat against the other point of the star, lower the presser foot, raise the needle and adjust the fabric beneath so that it lies flat and even. Put the needle back into the fabric at the same point it came out and continue sewing to the point of the star. Press the seam under the star. Repeat this process until you have added all six diamonds (Diagram 7). Set the whole star aside while you construct the rest of the quilt top.

10 Following the Assembly diagram, row by row, inset-piece the background diamonds to the stars in the order shown, using the same technique as for the whole star.

11 When you have pieced all the rows, join the rows together until you have completed the quilt top. Sew the corner quarter-diamonds in last. Press and check to make sure the quilt top is square before continuing.

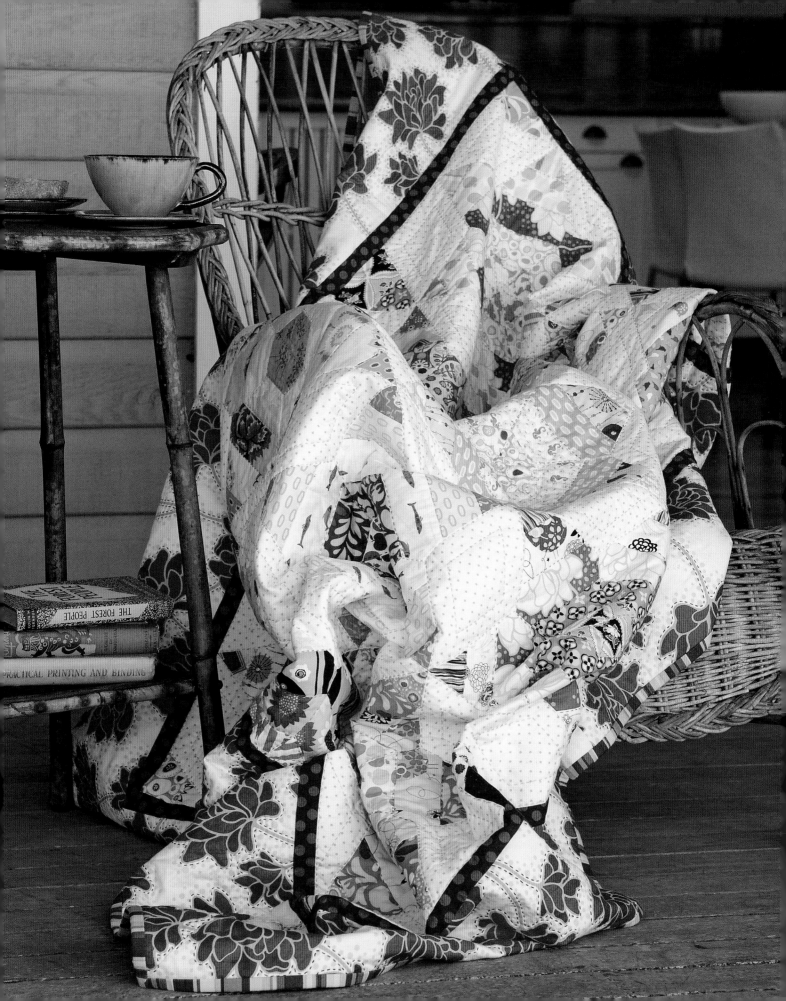

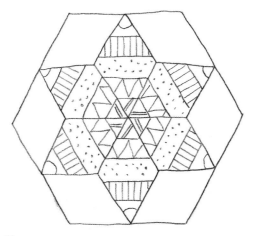

Diagram 7

Inner border

12 Sew all the strips for the Inner Border together into one long strip and press the seams to one side.

13 Measure your quilt through the centre across the width. Cut two pieces from the border strip to exactly this measurement.

14 Find the centre of a short side of the quilt top and the centre of one of the borders. Pin the centres together, then pin the ends together and pin in between. Sew as pinned. Repeat with the other short border. Press the seams towards the border.

15 Measure your quilt top through the centre again to get the long measurement. Cut the two border strips to your measurement. Attach the remaining borders as before. Press the seams towards the border.

Outer border

16 Sew the Outer Border strips together, end to end, into four pairs.

17 Measure your quilt through the centre to get the width. Cut two of the border strips to this measurement plus 16 inches, to allow for mitred corners.

18 Find the centre of a short side of the quilt top and the centre of one of the Outer Borders. Pin the centres together. Mark the border at 8½ inches in from the ends of the border strip, and pin this mark to the end of the quilt top at both ends. Pin in between, easing if needed. Begin sewing ¼ inch in from the edge of the quilt top, and finish the seam ¼ inch in from the opposite edge. Sew and repeat with the other short border. Press.

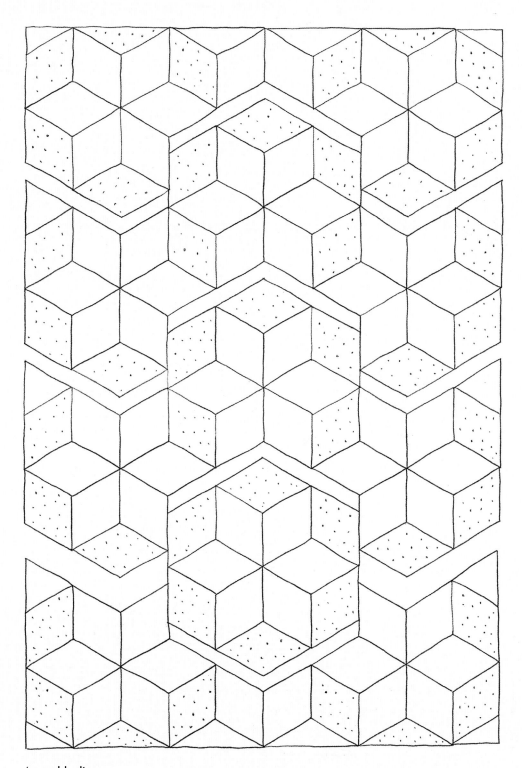

Assembly diagram

19 Measure and attach the long borders in the same way. (Remember to add the extra 16 inches to allow for mitred corners.)

20 Using the 45-degree angle on your patchwork ruler, rule a 45-degree angle across the corners of the borders. Sew the corners together along the 45-degree angle and check that the border will lie flat before trimming the excess fabric. Press the mitred seam open or to one side, and the border seam towards the border. Repeat with the other three corners. Your quilt top is complete.

{note on quilting}

I hand-quilted *Stars in Your Eyes* by outlining the diagonal lines in the diamonds using aqua perle cotton No 8. I then used 1-inch masking tape as a guide to quilt 1 inch inside the seam of all the diamonds. Finally, I outline-quilted all the seams in the stars using different coloured perle cotton No 8.

Backing, quilting and binding

Cut the backing fabric in half crosswise, giving two pieces, each 180 cm (72 inches) long. Trim the selvedges and sew the pieces together along the length to form one backing piece. Press the seam allowance open.

Refer to pages 190–199 for instructions on finishing.

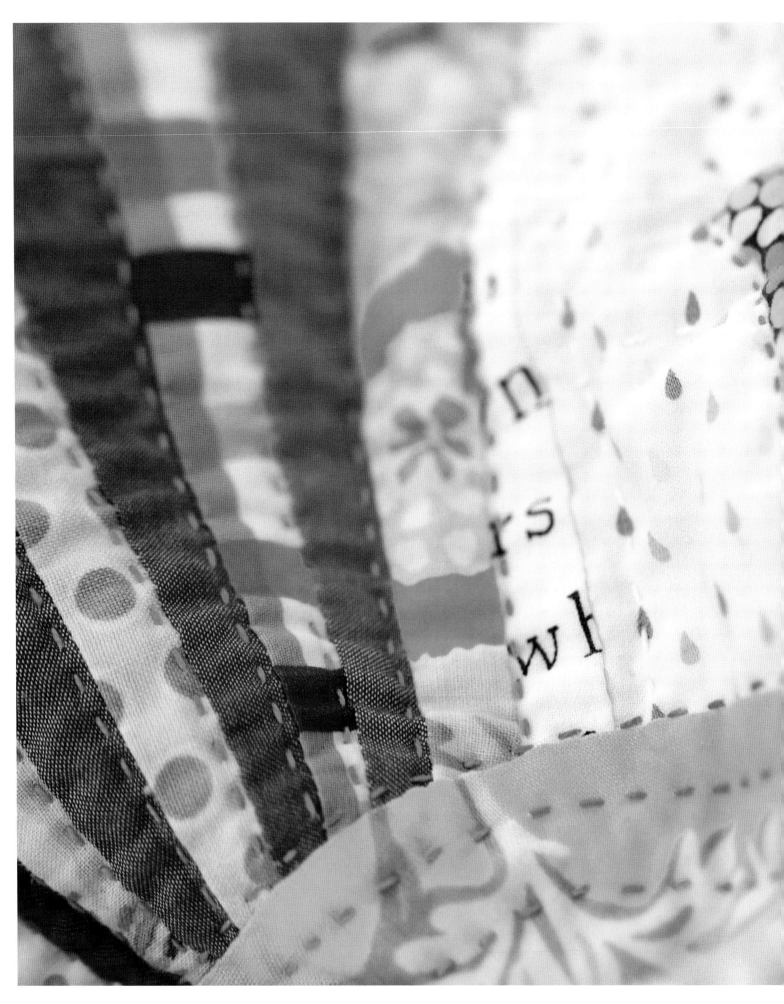

Needle-turn appliqué

A Little Silhouette
Dolly quilt, 42 cm (16½ inches) square

A Wing and a Prayer
Queen bed, 225 cm (88½ inches) square

A Wing and a Prayer is a four-block quilt, which is one traditional arrangement of antique American quilts. Making this quilt will give you the experience of working with large appliqué pieces and backgrounds. If you haven't used my appliqué technique before, making *A Little Silhouette* will try your skills at needle-turn appliqué, with inside and outside curves and points.

A Little Silhouette

Here is a little eagle: there's no mistaking his silhouette. His shadowy outline reminds me of a Pennsylvania Dutch Scherenschnitte, or paper cutting, although a very simple one.

The art of silhouette cutting was brought to America in the eighteenth century from central Europe. Although in its original European form it was very intricate, it was often simplified in American folk art. I think the positive and negative shapes created by silhouette cutting make wonderful graphic quilts. Why not try cutting your own silhouettes to appliqué?

Finished quilt size
Dolly quilt, 42 cm (16½ inches) square

Degree of difficulty **

MATERIALS AND TOOLS

- 36 scraps, at least 2½ inches square, in different pastels for background

- 30 cm (12 inches) spotted black fabric for Eagle and Border

- 25 cm (10 inches) green fabric for binding

- 1 fat quarter for backing

- 50 cm (20 inches) square cotton batting

- Black cotton thread for appliqué and hand quilting

- Template plastic

- 2B pencil

- Appliqué glue

- Straw needles for appliqué

- Silver gel pen

- Quilting needles ('betweens')

- General sewing and patchwork supplies (see page 22)

TEMPLATE

Trace the Eagle template (on pattern sheet) onto template plastic with a sharp 2B pencil and cut out accurately using sharp scissors (but not your fabric scissors).

CUTTING

All fabrics are strip-cut across the width of the fabric from fold to selvedge unless otherwise specified or unless you are using a directional print.

FROM SCRAP FABRICS, CUT:
- 36 squares, each 2½ inches, for the background.

FROM SPOTTED BLACK FABRIC, CUT:
- One Eagle shape. Place the Eagle template onto the right side of the black fabric and trace around it, using the gel pen. Cut the shape out using small, sharp scissors a scant ¼ inch from the gel pen line. Make sure to cut this first, so that you have a piece wide enough for the template.
- Three strips, 2½ inches wide x the remaining length of the fabric, for the Border. (You may, as I did, need to piece these strips to get enough length for your borders.)

FROM GREEN FABRIC, CUT:
- Three strips, 3 inches wide, for the binding.

Constructing the quilt top

Background

Make yourself a little design board by covering a piece of cardboard or similar with a leftover scrap of batting. This is very useful when you are piecing a block together and you don't want to lose track of your layout.

1 Lay the 2½-inch background squares out on the design board, or on a table, in six rows of six, to make a larger square containing 36 squares. Move the squares around until you are happy with the placement.

2 Pick the squares in the first row up in order and sew them into a strip of six squares. Put the strip back in the place it came from, so you don't lose track. Repeat with the other six strips of squares. Press the seams in each row in opposite directions, that is, Row 1 to the left, Row 2 to the right, Row 3 to the left, and so on (Diagram 1).

3 Using the pressed seams as a guide to get your points perfect, sew the rows together in order until your background is pieced. Press.

Appliqué

Read the instructions for Appliqué on page 186 before proceeding.

4 Fold your pieced background square into quarters to find the centre and finger-press the creases. Fold again on the diagonals and finger-press the creases. Using the wings and the tail of the eagle as a guide, centre the silhouette onto the background until you are happy with the placement (Diagram 2).

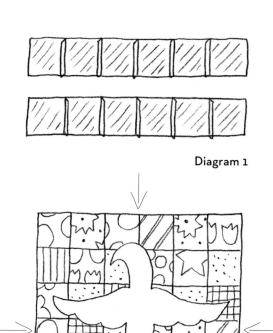

Diagram 1

Diagram 2

5 Lift the edges of the Eagle and put a drop of glue onto the fabric and press it down. Take care not to glue too close to the edge of the fabric or you will not be able to turn the edges under to appliqué. You only need a small spot of glue to make the piece stick. It will take a few moments to dry.

6 When the glue is dry and the shape is fused to the background, select a place on the shape on which to begin sewing. Do not begin on an inside curve or a point. Thread a straw needle with cotton to match the fabric you are appliquéing. Finger-press along the silver line all around the edge of the shape. Turn the edge under along the pressed line and sew the shape to the background using small stitches. You will need to clip into the inside curves to turn them under.

7 When you have completed the appliqué, press your block.

Border

8 From the 2½-inch border strips of black fabric, cut two pieces, each 12½ inches, and two pieces, each 16½ inches long. (If your fabric strips are not long enough to cut these strips from one piece, simply join them end to end until you have the required length.)

9 Find the centre of one side edge of the appliquéd square and the centre of one of the 12½-inch borders. Pin the centres together, then pin the ends. Pin in between, easing if needed. Sew, and repeat with the opposite border. Press.

10 Attach the two 16½-inch borders to the top and bottom edges of the quilt, as above. Press. Your quilt top is complete.

Backing, quilting and binding

Using masking tape, tape the backing fabric, face down, onto a table, smoothing out any creases as you go. Lay the batting piece onto the backing, and then the quilt top on top. Smooth any creases and hand-baste the three layers together using large stitches and working from the centre out. As this is only a small quilt, it does not need a lot of basting. The backing and batting should be larger than the top for ease of quilting; don't be tempted to trim them back.

Refer to pages 190–199 for instructions on finishing.

{note on quilting}

I hand-quilted *A Little Silhouette* using black sewing cotton. I echo-quilted around the eagle, in lines approximately ¼ inch apart, all over the background, and quilted lines, ¼ inch apart, in the border.

A Wing and a Prayer

The symbol of an eagle is often found in American antique quilts. I have always loved these quilts and wanted to make one, however, as I'm not American, I thought perhaps a fantasy bird of paradise might be more appropriate. This quilt is fun to make and the large appliqué shapes and bright fabrics make the sewing go quickly.

When choosing backgrounds, don't be afraid to choose fabrics with bolder, more interesting graphics. I feel that the newsprint fabric really makes this quilt more interesting.

Degree of difficulty ***

Finished quilt size
Queen bed, 225 cm (88½ inches) square

MATERIALS AND TOOLS

- 1 m (1⅛ yards) each of 4 different white fabrics for backgrounds, sashing and Borders 1 and 3

- 25 cm (10 inches) each of pink and tangerine linen for birds' Heads

- 50 cm (20 inches) each of aqua-patterned fabric and yellow-patterned fabric for birds' Wings and Bodies

- 20 cm (8 inches) turquoise-patterned fabric for birds' Eyes and Feet

- 20 cm (8 inches) each of 8 different plain red, pink and orange fabrics for birds' Tails and Border 2

- 10 cm (4 inches) each of 8 different pink, yellow and aqua printed fabrics for birds' Tails and Border 2

- 20 cm (8 inches) pink-and-yellow spotted fabric for Stars

- 20 cm (8 inches) teal-and-pink floral fabric for Circles

- Scrap of pink fabric for Inner Circle

- 65 cm (26 inches) blue-and-green spotted fabric for Border 4 and Outer Star

- 40 cm (16 inches) red-striped or dark-pink-striped fabric for Border 4

- 1.7 m (1⅞ yards) multicoloured-spotted fabric for Border 5
- 75 cm (30 inches) bright-pink-striped fabric for binding
- 5.5 m (6 yards) backing fabric
- 235 cm (92 inches) square cotton batting
- Cotton threads to match appliqué fabrics
- Several large sheets of template plastic
- 2B pencil
- Appliqué glue
- Straw needles for appliqué
- Silver gel pen
- Perle cotton No 8 in white, pink, orange and variegated for hand-quilting
- No 9 crewel embroidery needles for quilting
- General sewing and patchwork supplies (see page 22)

TEMPLATES

Trace Templates A (Head), B (Body), C (Wing), D (Foot), E (Eye), F (Wedge Tail), G (Outer Star), H (Outer Circle), I (Inner Star), J (Inner Circle), K (Half-Circle) and L (Half-Star) (on pattern sheets), onto template plastic with a sharp 2B pencil and cut out accurately using sharp scissors (but not your fabric scissors). Label all the pieces and be sure to label Templates C and D 'right side up'.

CUTTING

All fabrics are strip-cut across the width of the fabric from fold to selvedge unless otherwise specified or unless you are using a directional print. When cutting the appliqué shapes, place the template on the right side of the fabric and trace around it with the gel pen. Cut the shapes out using small, sharp scissors, a scant ¼ inch from the gel pen line. Use a ruler to rule a ¼-inch seam along the top edge only of each Wedge Tail shape.

FROM EACH OF THE FOUR WHITE BACKGROUND FABRICS, CUT:

- Four squares, each 12½ inches, for appliqué backgrounds (16 squares in total).

Cut all of the remaining fabric into 4½-inch wide strips, for the sashing and Borders 1 and 3, and set aside.

FROM EACH OF THE PINK AND TANGERINE LINENS, CUT:

- Two Template A Eagle Head (four Heads in total).

FROM EACH OF THE YELLOW-PATTERNED AND AQUA-PATTERNED FABRICS, CUT:

- Two Template B Body (four Bodies in total).
- Two Template C Wing, right side up (four Wings in total).
- Two Template C Wing, right side down (four Wings in total).

FROM THE TURQUOISE-PATTERNED FABRIC, CUT:
- Four Template D Foot, right side up.
- Four Template D Foot, right side down.
- Four Template E Eye.

FROM EACH OF THE PLAIN RED, ORANGE AND PINK FABRICS, CUT:
- Four Template F Wedge Tail (32 Wedge Tails in total).

Cut all the remaining fabric into $1\frac{1}{2}$-inch strips for Border 2 and set aside.

FROM EACH OF THE ASSORTED PINK, YELLOW AND AQUA PRINTED FABRICS, CUT:
- Four Template F Wedge Tail (32 Wedge Tails in total).

Cut all the remaining fabric into $1\frac{1}{2}$-inch strips for Border 2 and set aside.

FROM PINK-AND-YELLOW SPOT, CUT:
- One Template I Inner Star.
- Four Template L Half-Star.

FROM TEAL-AND-PINK FLORAL FABRIC, CUT:
- One Template H Outer Circle.
- Four Template K Half-Circle.

FROM PINK SCRAP, CUT:
- One Template J Inner Circle.

FROM BLUE-AND-GREEN SPOTTED FABRIC, CUT:
- One Template G Outer Star.
- 10 strips, $1\frac{1}{2}$ inches wide, for Border 4.

FROM RED-STRIPED FABRIC, CUT:
- 10 strips, $1\frac{1}{2}$ inches wide, for Border 4.

FROM MULTICOLOURED-SPOTTED FABRIC, CUT:
- Eight strips, $6\frac{1}{2}$ inches wide, for Border 5.

FROM BRIGHT-PINK-STRIPED BINDING FABRIC, CUT:
- 10 strips, 3 inches wide, for binding.

Constructing the quilt top

Background blocks (make 4)

1 Sew the 16 white background 12½-inch squares into pairs, making sure to mix the patterns. Press the seams to one side.

2 Join two of the pairs along the length to make a four-patch block. Repeat to make four blocks in this manner. Press.

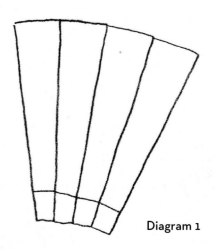

Diagram 1

Wedge tails (make 4)

3 Arrange the 64 Wedge Tail shapes into four sets of 16, alternating eight plain and eight patterned fabrics until you are happy with the arrangement. Sew the Wedges together along the long side in order (Diagram 1), and press the seams under the plain fabrics. Make four Wedge Tails.

Appliqué

Read the instructions for Appliqué on page 186 before proceeding. The birds are appliquéd first, and the Star and Half-Stars are appliquéd in place when the sashing and Border 1 have been added.

4 Fold one of your four-patch background squares in half on the diagonal and finger-press the crease. Repeat across the other diagonal. Using the photograph and the seams and diagonal creases as a guide, arrange the pieces of a bird onto the background until you are happy with the positioning. Remember that the edges of the Wings, Tail and Feet will go under the Body.

5 Lift the edges of the fabrics, put a drop of glue onto the fabrics and press them down. Take care not to glue too close to the edge of the fabrics or you will not be able to turn the edges under to appliqué. You only need a small spot of glue to make the pieces stick. They will take a few moments to dry.

6 When the glue is dry and the shapes are fused to the background, select a shape on which to begin sewing. Thread a straw needle with cotton to match the fabric you are appliquéing. Finger-press along the silver line all around the edge of the shape. Turn the edge under along the pressed line and sew the shape to the background, using small stitches. You will need to clip into the inside curves to turn them under.

7 When you have appliquéd these shapes, turn the block over to the back. Select a shape and carefully pinch the background fabric away from the appliqué fabric on the front. Make a small cut, using small scissors, and carefully cut the background away from behind the appliqué, approximately ¼ inch from the seam lines (Diagram 2). I do not usually cut my backgrounds away, but due to the large size of these shapes, I have done so to make quilting on the appliqué easier.

8 Press the block, and trim to square it up, if necessary, to be 24½ inches square. Repeat until you have completed four blocks.

Sashing (white)

9 From the 4½-inch wide strips of white fabric for sashing and Borders 1 and 3, cut each long piece into two random lengths. For example, if the strip is 44 inches long, you might remove the selvedges, then cut a 20-inch strip and a 23-inch strip. Repeat with all of the fabrics, so that there are several different lengths. You do not need

{tip}

This glue is designed to be removable. If you put something in the wrong place you can peel it back and reposition it, and after your appliqué is finished, it washes out.

Diagram 2

to measure, just cut. Next, sew all the 4½-inch border strips together, end to end, into one long strip. This makes your sashing and borders appear random. Press.

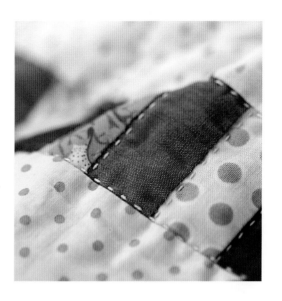

10 Arrange your Bird blocks on a design wall or the floor, in their correct positions with their heads towards the centre, so that you do not get confused when piecing them together.

11 Cut two pieces from the border strip, each 24½ inches long, for sashing. Sew a sashing strip between the two upper Bird blocks (Diagram 3), then repeat for the two lower Bird blocks. Press the seams under the appliqué squares.

12 Cut another sashing piece, 52½ inches long. Find the centre of the top strip of birds and the centre of the sashing strip. Pin the centres together, then pin the ends. Pin in between, easing if needed. Sew. Repeat this process to add the bottom strip of birds to the lower edge of the sashing. Press.

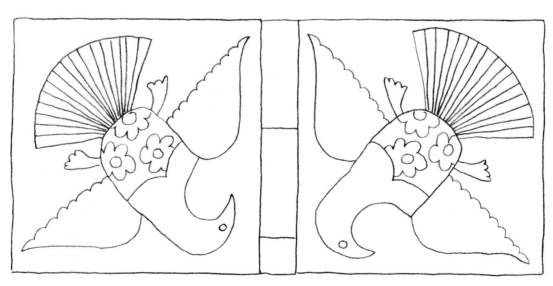

Diagram 3

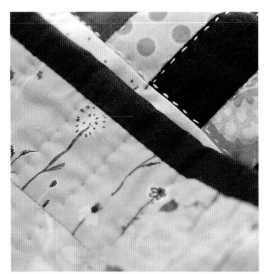

Centre star appliqué

13 Centre Template G (Outer Star) into the space between the blocks and glue. The shape will overlap the sashing and the corners of the blocks. Sew, then add, in layers, Template H (Outer Circle), then Template I (Inner Star), then Template J (Inner Circle) at the centre of the star. After you sew each layer, turn the block over and cut the fabric away from behind the shape you just sewed, using small sharp scissors, about $\frac{1}{4}$ inch away from the sewing line. This will stop the appliqué from becoming too bulky.

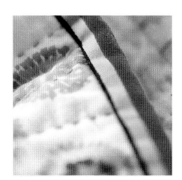

Border 1 (white)

14 From the long white border strip, cut two more strips, each 52½ inches long. Pin one to the top of the quilt as for Step 12, and sew. Repeat with the bottom edge.

15 For the side borders, cut two pieces, each 60½ inches long. Sew these borders to either side of the quilt top, as above. Press the seams under the appliquéd blocks.

Outer star appliqué

16 When you have sewn the border pieces on, find and mark the centre of each border. Finger-press each Template K (Half-Circle) in half to find the centre, match this point to the halfway point on the border and glue the four Half-Circles in place. Appliqué the Half-Circles in position, cut away the excess fabric from the back, then add the four Template L (Half-Stars) on top.

Border 2 (pieced)

17 Take all the 1½-inch strips you cut from the remaining eagle Tail fabrics. Sew them together lengthwise in rows of eight, alternating a plain fabric with a patterned fabric (Diagram 4). Press all the seams to one side. Repeat with all the fabrics until you have sewn them into 8-strip sets, alternating and mixing the groupings of fabrics. Press.

18 Trim the end of one 8-strip set to be square, and cross-cut into strips, 2½ inches wide. Repeat until you have cut all of the 8-strip sets into 2½-inch pieces (Diagram 5).

19 When you have cut all the pieces, sew them together along the short edge to make long strips, 2½ inches wide. You will need two strips, 60½ inches long, and two strips, 64½ inches long.

20 Repeating the steps to attach borders, detailed in Step 12 above, pin the 60½-inch strips to the top and bottom of the quilt and sew. Repeat with the 64½-inch strips on either side of the quilt top. Press the seams under the white borders.

Border 3 (white)

21 Take the remaining white 4½-inch strip and cut two pieces, each 64½ inches long. Sew these to the top and bottom of the quilt. Cut another two pieces, each 72½ inches long and sew these to the top sides of the quilt. Press the seams under the white borders.

Border 4 (pieced)

22 Sew together lengthwise the red-striped and blue-and-green spot fabrics into sets of 6 strips, alternating the fabrics as you go. You should have three sets of six strips each, and one set of only two strips.

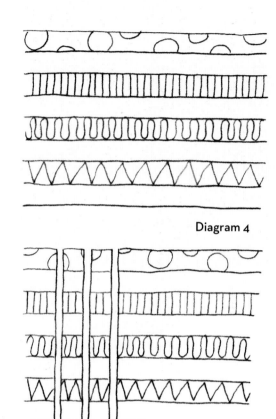

Diagram 4

Diagram 5

23 Cross-cut the sets into 2½-inch strips, as for Border 2. Join the strips, end to end, to make two strips, 72½ inches long, and two strips, 76½ inches long. Attach the shorter strips to the top and bottom of the quilt and the longer strips to the sides. Press the seams under the white borders.

Border 5 (multicoloured spots)

24 Remove the selvedges and sew all of the Border 5 strips together, end to end, into one long strip. From this strip, cut two pieces, 76½ inches long, and two pieces, 88½ inches long. Sew to the top and bottom and sides of the quilt, as above. Press the seams under the white borders. Your quilt top is complete.

{note on quilting}

I hand-quilted *A Wing and a Prayer* **using perle cotton No 8. I outline-quilted all the appliqué using pink or orange, and quilted a grid pattern in the backgrounds, 2 inches apart, using white. I then quilted the outer borders, using variegated perle cotton.**

Backing, quilting and binding

From the backing fabric, cut two pieces 244 cm (96 inches long) and three pieces, 20 cm (8 inches) wide. Sew the 20 cm (8-inch) pieces together, end to end, into one long strip. From this strip, cut a piece 244 cm (96 inches) long. Remove the selvedges and stitch the pieces together up the long seams. Press the seam allowance open and press the backing piece carefully.

Refer to pages 190–199 for instructions on finishing.

Using wedges

Fanfare

Dolly quilt, 47 cm (18½ inches) square

Hanging Lanterns

Queen size, 222 x 243 cm (87½ x 95½ inches)

A wedge ruler is one of the most exciting patchwork tools I own. Just when I think I know everything it can do, it surprises me again. Here, you can use wedge shapes to make the little fans in the fanfare quilt, and also try out some needle-turn appliqué if you haven't tried it before.

Hanging Lanterns is a more complex use of a Dresden Plate wedge. There is a lot of piecing and appliqué in this quilt, but the results are spectacular.

Although the sewing in these quilts can be a little tricky, if you are careful and keep your seams accurate you should be fine. The magic of both these blocks is that if you do have to make your lanterns or fans a little flatter, you can pleat them slightly at the centre and then cover the pleat with the appliqué, but shhh...don't tell anyone I told you!

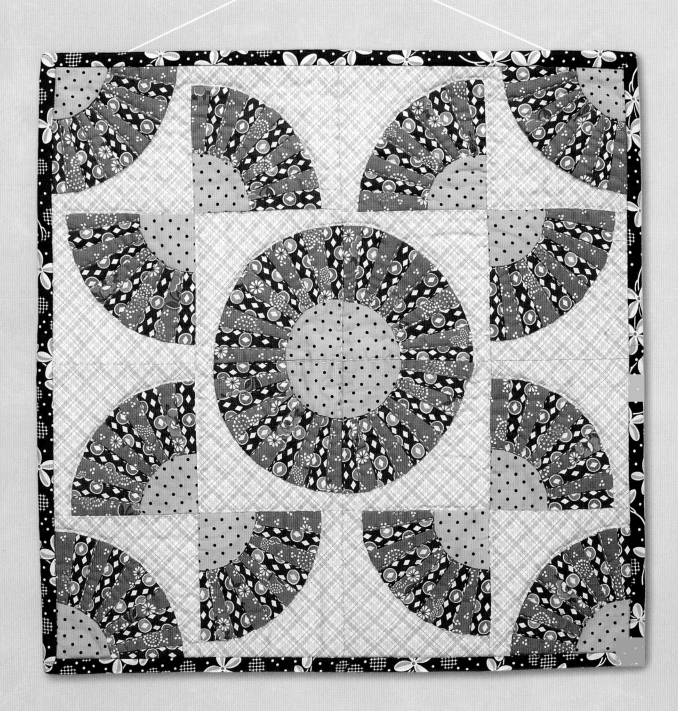

Fanfare

Fans are a fantastic graphic shape in quilts. Different placement of them can create a quilt full of movement and interest. You may like to make all your fan blocks and then play with different configurations of them before you sew them together.

Finished quilt size
Dolly quilt, 47 cm (18½ inches) square

Degree of difficulty ***

MATERIALS AND TOOLS

- 20 cm (8 inches) each of two different contrasting purple fabrics for fans
- 25 cm (10 inches) pink/green/white checked fabric for background
- 10 cm (4 inches) spotted green fabric for fan centres
- 25 cm (10 inches) dark-purple fabric for binding
- 60 cm (24 inches) for backing
- 60 cm (24 inches) square cotton batting
- Purple cotton thread for appliqué
- Template plastic
- Sharp 2B pencil and silver gel pen
- Appliqué glue
- Straw needles for appliqué
- Silver gel pen
- White perle cotton No 8 for hand-quilting

- No 9 crewel embroidery needles for quilting
- General sewing and patchwork supplies (see page 22)

TEMPLATES
Trace Templates A, B and C (on pattern sheet) onto template plastic with a sharp 2B pencil and cut out using sharp scissors (but not your fabric scissors).

CUTTING
All fabrics are strip-cut across the width of the fabric from fold to selvedge unless otherwise specified or unless you are using a directional print.

FROM PINK/GREEN/WHITE CHECKED FABRIC, CUT:
- Two strips, 5 inches wide. Cross-cut these strips into 16 squares, each 5 inches, for the background.

FROM EACH OF THE TWO PURPLE FABRICS, CUT:
- Two strips, 3 inches wide, for the fans. Cross-cut these strips into 80 fan blades (from each fabric), using Template A (160 fan blades in total).

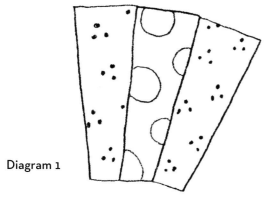

Diagram 1

FROM SPOTTED GREEN FABRIC, CUT:
- 16 fan centres, using Template B.

FROM DARK-PURPLE FABRIC, CUT:
- Three strips, 3 inches wide, and set aside for binding.

Constructing the quilt top

Fans

1 Sew together a set of 10 fan blades, five of each fabric, along the long side of the blades. Begin at the left-hand side of the fan and start with a light purple blade (Diagram 1). Make sure that all your blades are sewn in the same order. Press all the seams to one side. Continue in this manner until you have made 16 fans.

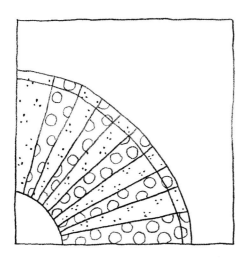

Diagram 2

Appliqué

Read the instructions for Appliqué on page 186 before proceeding.

2 Using a patchwork ruler and silver gel pen, draw a line ¼ inch from the outside edge of the fan (Diagram 2).

3 Place a fan onto a pink/green/white background square by lining up the long edges of the fan with the edges of the square (Diagram 3).

4 Lift the edges of the fan and put a drop of appliqué glue onto the back of the fabric and press it down. Take care not to glue too close to the edge of the fabric or you will not be able to turn the edges under to appliqué. You only need a small spot of glue to make the piece stick. It will take a few moments to dry.

Diagram 3

5 When all the fans are fused to the backgrounds, begin sewing along the outside edge of the fan to appliqué the fan to the background. Finger-press along the silver line around the edge of the shape, then turn the edge under and sew along the pressed line using small stitches. Repeat with all 16 fans.

6 Place Template C in the corner of the Template B fan centre shapes and draw the seam allowance on, using the gel pen (Diagram 4).

7 Glue the fan centres into the corner of the background squares and appliqué the curved edge, as above. Complete all 16 blocks in this way.

8 Press your blocks and ensure they are 5 inches square. Trim if necessary.

Assembling the quilt top

9 Lay all the blocks out onto a table or design board, referring to the photograph for placement.

10 Sew the blocks together into rows of four, then sew the four rows together. Take care to match the seams and the edges of the fans and fan corners. Press. Your quilt top is complete.

Backing, quilting and binding

Using masking tape, tape the backing fabric, face down, onto a table, smoothing out any creases as you go. Lay the batting piece onto the backing, and then the quilt top on top. Smooth any creases and hand-baste the three layers together using large stitches and working from the centre out. The backing and batting should be larger than the top for ease of quilting; don't be tempted to trim them back.

Refer to pages 190–199 for instructions on finishing.

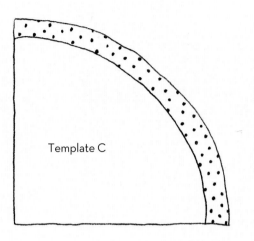

Template C

Diagram 4

{note on quilting}

I hand-quilted *Fanfare* using white perle cotton No 8, echo-quilting around the fans and the fan centres.

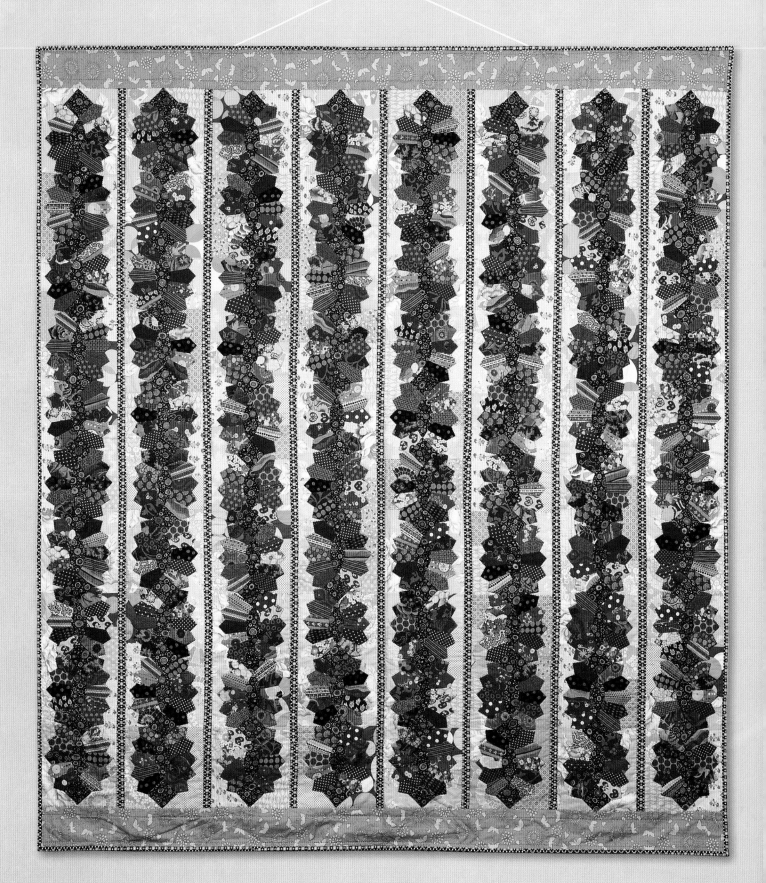

Hanging Lanterns

Designing this quilt, I had an image of a Chinese garden at dusk, the sun going down, making soft shadows and pastel colours in the plants. Bunches of red paper lanterns hang in the trees, glowing pink and orange and inviting you to come for a walk.

When I was choosing backgrounds I was very careful to choose fabrics that would not jump out and spoil the effect of the red lanterns. All the lantern fabrics are strong and able to hold their own against the backgrounds.

Finished quilt size
Queen size 222 x 243 cm (87½ x 95½ inches)

Degree
of difficulty
****

MATERIALS AND TOOLS

- 90 cm (1 yard) each of six different grey and pale-blue fabrics for backgrounds

- 1.5 m (1⅝ yards) dark-grey fabric for sashing strips and binding

- 10 cm (4 inches) each of a wide selection of red and dark-pink fabrics for lanterns, totalling 5.3 m (5¾ yards), OR use half-metres (half-yards) of 11 different fabrics for simplicity

- 2.8 m (3 yards) brown fabric for 'eyes' and setting squares

- 65 cm (26 inches) grey-patterned fabric for top and bottom borders

- 8 m (8⅔ yards) backing fabric

- 265 x 260 cm (98 x 104 inches) cotton batting

- 18-degree wedge ruler (optional, see page 29)

- 2B pencil

- Template plastic

- Silver gel pen

- Appliqué glue

- Straw needles for appliqué

- Medium-pink and brown cotton thread to match appliqué fabrics

- Perle cotton No 8 in brown and red for hand quilting

- No 9 crewel embroidery needles for quilting

- General sewing and patchwork supplies (see page 22)

TEMPLATES

Trace Templates A and B (on pattern sheet) onto template plastic with a sharp 2B pencil and cut out accurately using sharp scissors (but not your fabric scissors). If you are using an 18-degree wedge ruler, you will not need Template B.

CUTTING

All fabrics are strip-cut across the width of the fabric from fold to selvedge unless otherwise specified or unless you are using a directional print.

FROM EACH OF THE GREY AND PALE-BLUE BACKGROUND FABRICS, CUT:

- Two strips, 6½ inches wide. Cross-cut these strips into 12 squares, each 6½ inches (72 squares in total).
- Five strips, 4½ inches wide. Cross-cut three of these strips into 10½-inch pieces, to yield 12 rectangles, each 4½ x 10½ inches (72 rectangles in total). Cross-cut remaining two strips into 6½-inch pieces, to yield 12 rectangles, each 4½ x 6½ inches (72 rectangles in total).

FROM DARK-GREY FABRIC, CUT:

- 14 strips, 1½ inches wide, for sashing.
- 11 strips, 3 inches wide, for binding.

FROM THE RED AND DARK-PINK FABRICS, CUT:

- 50 strips, 4 inches wide. Using either Template B or the 2-inch line on the 18-degree ruler, cut a total of 800 plate blades. (You can cut approximately 16 blades from each fabric.)

FROM BROWN FABRIC, CUT:

- Nine strips, 4½ inches wide. Cross-cut these strips into 80 squares, each 4½ inches. Set remaining fabric aside for appliqué.

FROM GREY-PATTERNED FABRIC, CUT:

- Five strips, 5 inches wide, for the Top and Bottom Borders.

Constructing the quilt top

Background blocks
(make 64 blocks + 8 half–blocks)

The background is made up of vertical rows of blocks. Each full block contains a 6½-inch square, a 4½ x 6½-inch rectangle and a 4½ x 10½-inch rectangle. Choose the pieces for a block, taking care not to choose two fabrics the same.

Diagram 1
Full block

1 Sew the 4½ x 6½-inch rectangle to the side of the 6½-inch square. Finger-press the seam towards the 4½-inch piece. Sew the 10½ x 4½-inch rectangle to the long side of this unit (Diagram 1). Press and repeat to make 64 full blocks.

Diagram 2
Half block

2 Make eight half-blocks by sewing the remaining 6½-inch squares to the remaining 4½ x 6½-inch rectangles (Diagram 2).

3 Lay out all of the blocks on your design wall in eight vertical rows of nine blocks. Each vertical row should contain eight full blocks and one half-block. You can alternate where you place the half-block within each row.

4 Turn the blocks a half-turn around as you move down the rows, so that they look random. Mix the blocks until you are happy with the placement, and then sew the blocks into vertical rows. Each finished row should be 86½ inches long (including seam allowance).

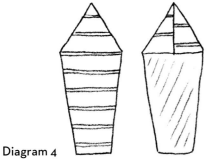

Diagram 3

Diagram 4

Hanging lanterns

5 First, sew the lantern 'blades'. Fold each of the wedges in half lengthwise, with right sides together, and sew along the top (longer) edge using a ¼-inch seam (Diagram 3). This is an excellent time to chain piece— there are a lot of wedges!

6 Turn the edges right side out, taking care to poke the point out so it is nice and sharp. Press the wedges flat, with the seam at the back aligning with the centre line of the wedge (Diagram 4).

7 Sew the wedges together along the long raw edges into sets of five wedges, forming an arc (Diagram 5), mixing the fabrics well. Repeat until you have sewn together 160 arcs.

8 Place an arc face down onto the right side of a 4½-inch brown square, ¼ inch from the corner (Diagram 6). Sew. Place another arc on the other side of the square in a similar manner and sew (Diagram 7). Press the seams towards the arcs.

Diagram 5

Diagram 6

Diagram 7

Diagram 8

9 Repeat this step at the opposite end of the arc. Depending on how accurate your cutting and piecing has been at the wedge stage, you may find that the arc does not lie perfectly flat—this can easily be fixed at the appliqué stage so don't worry too much!

10 Next join an arc to either side of the second square. The corner of the square will be visible at the point where the arc meets (Diagram 8). Press.

11 Repeat in this manner until you have created a chain of 10 hanging lanterns, beginning and ending with a square. Make eight chains of 10 hanging lanterns like this.

Appliqué

Read the instructions for Appliqué on page 186 before proceeding.

12 Place the Template A shape onto the right side of the reserved brown fabric and trace around it with the silver gel pen. Cut out the shape, approximately ¼ inch outside the gel pen line. Repeat to cut a total of 80 Template A shapes.

13 Take a vertical background row and press it in half along the length to make a line down the centre. Lay it out on the floor or a large table. Using the ironed crease as a guide, centre a strip of lanterns down the background strip, making sure that the corners of the squares on the ends of the strip are touching the top and bottom edges of the backgrounds.

14 Lift the edges of the lantern shapes and put a drop of appliqué glue onto the appliqué fabrics and press them down. You only need a small amount of glue to make the pieces stick. They will take a few moments to dry.

15 When the glue is dry and the arcs are stuck to the background, take an eye-shaped Template A piece and place it over the centre hole in the first lantern. Position the eye by using a pin through the point of the eye at the gel pen line and lining it up with the seams on the lanterns. When the eye is in position, glue it in place, taking care not to glue too close to the edge, so that you can turn the edges of the shape under.

16 Thread your straw needle with a medium-pink cotton. Sew along the edges of the arcs using small stitches. When you reach the point where the brown square is showing between the arcs, tuck it underneath the seams using your needle to hide it and keep sewing. Continue sewing around all the arcs.

17 Thread your needle with brown cotton. Finger-press along the silver line all around the edge of the first eye shape. Turn the edge under along the pressed line and sew the eye to the lantern using small stitches.

18 Repeat until you have sewed all the arcs and eyes to the background strips. Press.

Sashing

19 Piece all the 1½-inch strips of dark grey fabric together into one long strip, first removing the selvedges, if you have not already done so. Press. From this strip, cut seven strips, 1½ inches wide x 86½ inches long. (Adjust this measurement if your lantern strips are not 86½ inches long.)

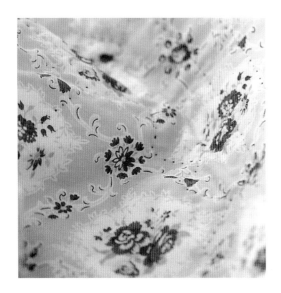

20 Sew all of the lantern strips together with grey sashing strips in between, beginning and ending with a lantern strip. Be sure to find the centre of a lantern strip, the centre of a grey sashing strip and pin; then pin the ends and pin in between, easing as you go, before you sew. This will prevent any waves in your long strips. Press.

Borders

21 Sew together all of the 5-inch grey-patterned strips, end to end, to make one long strip. Measure your quilt top through the centre to get the true width. It should measure 87½ inches. Cut a Top and Bottom border strip to this length.

22 Find the centre of the top of the quilt top and the centre of one strip and pin. Pin the ends, then pin in between, easing as you go, if needed. Sew and repeat with the bottom border. Press. Your quilt top is complete.

Backing, quilting and binding

Cut the backing fabric into three pieces, each 265 cm (104 inches) long. Remove the selvedges and stitch the pieces together up the long seams. Press the seam allowance open and press the backing piece carefully.

Refer to pages 190–199 for instructions on finishing.

{note on quilting}

I hand-quilted *Hanging Lanterns* using perle cotton No 8. I outline-quilted around the lanterns using red, and outlined the squares using dark brown.

Step-down piecing

A Step Down
Dolly quilt, 39 cm (15½ inches) square

The Night Garden
Throw or single bed topper,
137 x 163 cm (54 x 64 inches)

If you have never done this kind of piecing before, I strongly
recommend that you make the dolly quilt before you attempt
The Night Garden. It's not that the sewing in the quilt is difficult
as such, only that the idea of leaving the seams open and working
out where each piece goes next can be quite confusing. Making
the dolly quilt will give you the confidence to set your
pieced tulips into your night garden with ease.

A Step Down

I used a square of some of my favourite novelty fabrics for this quilt. Anyone who has ever had a peek in my stash knows my fondness for fabrics with little animals on them, so this quilt has only used a very tiny part of a big load of fabric. It's hard to know which is my favourite, but I am very fond of elephants!

This pattern makes a wonderful larger quilt too. Double the size of your squares and sew until the quilt seems large enough, then add the border rectangles. Sometimes simple is wonderful.

Finished quilt size
Dolly quilt, 39 cm (15½ inches) square

Degree of difficulty **

MATERIALS AND TOOLS

- 10-cm (4-inch) square of 24 different novelty prints with light backgrounds, or scrap

- 10 cm (4 inches) dark-brown fabric for accent squares

- 15 cm (6 inches) dark-blue patterned fabric for binding

- 1 fat quarter for backing

- 50 cm (20 inches) square cotton batting

- White and brown perle cotton No 8 for hand-quilting

- No 9 crewel embroidery needles for quilting

- General sewing and patchwork supplies (see page 22)

CUTTING

All fabrics are strip-cut across the width of the fabric from fold to selvedge unless otherwise specified or unless you are using a directional print.

FROM THE 24 SQUARES OF NOVELTY FABRIC, CUT:
- 16 squares, each 3½ inches.
- 8 rectangles, 3½ x 2 inches, for edges.

FROM DARK-BROWN FABRIC, CUT:
- One strip, 2 inches wide. Cross-cut into 20 squares, each 2 inches.

FROM DARK-BLUE BINDING FABRIC, CUT:
- Two strips, 3 inches wide. Set aside for binding.

Diagram 1 ••• = seam left open

Constructing the quilt top

This quilt is put together in an interesting manner. Due to the step-downs in the pattern, it cannot be sewn together in a straight line, or in rows. You will need a design board or similar flat surface to lay out the quilt on, so that you do not get mixed up.

1 Referring to the photograph, lay the large and small squares out according to the pattern. Don't worry too much about positioning until you have them all laid out, and then you can rearrange them until you are happy with the colour placement.

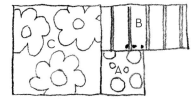

Diagram 2 ••• = seam left open

2 When you are pleased with the layout, begin sewing at the top left-hand corner. Sew brown square A to the bottom edge of rectangle B as shown in Diagram 1. Leave the end of the seam open by ½ inch. Turn the seam towards piece A.

Diagram 3

••• = seam left open

{tip}

Piecing a quilt top together in this way may seem very confusing at first, but the best way to learn is simply to do it. You will find that after you have done a few open and closed seams in this way, you will be just fine. As long as you remember that the quilt cannot be put together in the usual rows, everything will be OK!

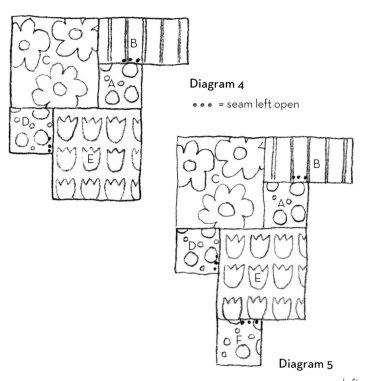

Diagram 4

••• = seam left open

Diagram 5

••• = seam left open

3 Sew the unit you have just created to the right-hand side of large square C in the top left-hand corner (Diagram 2). Finger-press the seam towards the brown square.

4 Sew brown square D to the left-hand top edge of large square E, again leaving the seam open at the lower end (Diagram 3). Turn the seam towards the brown fabric and sew this unit to the unit above (Diagram 4).

5 Next, sew brown square F to the bottom of large square E, leaving the end of the seam open, as shown (Diagram 5).

6 Sew edge piece G to the bottom of brown square D (Diagram 6), then close the open seam all the way from part-way down D to the bottom of G (Diagram 7).

7 Continue in this manner, until you have pieced all the squares together according to the photograph. Your quilt top is complete.

Backing, quilting and binding

Using masking tape, tape the backing fabric, face down, onto a table, smoothing out any creases as you go. Lay the batting piece onto the backing, and then the quilt top on top. Smooth any creases and hand-baste the three layers together using large stitches and working from the centre out. As this is only a small quilt, it does not need a lot of basting. The backing and batting should be larger than the top for ease of quilting; don't be tempted to trim them back.

Refer to pages 190–199 for instructions on finishing.

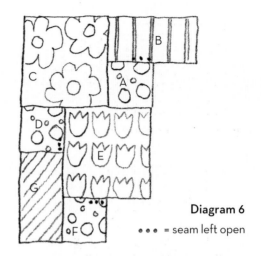

Diagram 6

• • • = seam left open

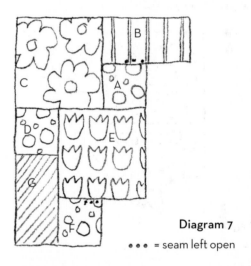

Diagram 7

• • • = seam left open

{note on quilting}

I hand-quilted *A Step Down*. I quilted a diamond shape into each large square using white perle cotton No 8 and an 'X' onto each brown square using dark brown.

The Night Garden

The scattering of bright flowers against the night-time backdrop makes the tulips seem like little jewels. The flowers are not hard to construct, but you must square them up carefully before you piece or everything will go wrong! Fabrics for this quilt need brightness, interest and pattern in the leaves for the flowers, or they won't stand out against the plain, dark backgrounds.

Finished quilt size
Throw or single bed topper
137 x 163 cm (54 x 64 inches)

Degree
of difficulty
****

MATERIALS AND TOOLS

- 2.1 m (2½ yards) plain dark-blue fabric for background

- 35 cm (14 inches) each of six plain dark-blue and -green fabrics for background

- 30 cm (12 inches) dark-blue-patterned fabric for setting rectangles

- 55 cm (22 inches) green-patterned fabric for setting rectangles and outer border

- Pink, orange, blue and yellow scraps totalling 85 cm (34 inches) for tulip flowers

- 10 cm each of five different lime-green fabrics for tulip leaves

- 55 cm (22 inches) striped fabric for binding

- 3.1 m (3½ yards) backing fabric

- 155 x 175 cm (64 x 70 inches) cotton batting

- Template plastic (optional)

- 2B pencil

- The Night Garden template set available at www.sarahfielke.com (optional, see page 210)

- General sewing and patchwork supplies (see page 22)

TEMPLATES

If you are not using the template set, trace Templates A, B and C (on pattern sheet) onto template plastic with a sharp 2B pencil and cut out accurately using sharp scissors (but not your fabric scissors). Mark the right side up on each template.

CUTTING

All fabrics are strip-cut across the width of the fabric from fold to selvedge unless otherwise specified or unless you are using a directional print.

FROM DARK-BLUE BACKGROUND FABRIC, CUT:

- Three strips, 5 inches wide. Cross-cut these strips into 24 rectangles, 4¼ x 5 inches, for plain blocks.
- 186 Template A shapes.
- 93 Template C triangles.
- 93 Template C Reversed triangles.

FROM EACH OF THE OTHER DARK-BLUE AND GREEN FABRICS, CUT:

- Three strips, 5 inches wide. Cross-cut these strips into 18 rectangles, 4¼ x 5 inches, for the plain blocks (you should have a total of 90 plain blocks from these fabrics). It is a good idea not to cut these blocks until you have completed your Tulip blocks. They need to be the same size.

{tip}

I recommend using a design wall for this quilt (see page 24).

FROM DARK-BLUE SETTING RECTANGLE FABRIC, CUT:

- Four strips, 2¾ inches wide. Cross-cut into 100 rectangles, 1¾ x 2¾ inches.

FROM DARK-GREEN-PATTERNED SETTING RECTANGLE FABRIC, CUT:

- Four strips, 2¾ inches wide. Cross-cut into 100 pieces, 1¾ x 2¾ inches.
- Six strips, 1½ inches wide, for the Borders.

FROM EACH OF THE LIME-GREEN FABRICS, CUT:

- 18 pairs of Template B triangles (180 triangles).
- From just three of the fabrics, cut an extra pair of B triangles (186 triangles or 93 pairs of 'tulip leaves' in total).

FROM THE SCRAP FABRICS, CUT:
- 93 Template A shapes, for the tulip tops.

FROM THE STRIPED BINDING FABRIC, CUT:
- Seven strips, 3 inches wide. Set aside for binding.

Constructing the quilt top

Tulip blocks (make 93)

1 To make one Tulip block, sew a dark blue Template A piece to either side of a coloured scrap Template A piece (Diagram 1). Trim the 'ear' from the top of the points and finger-press the seams under the coloured centre piece.

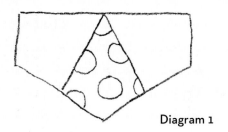

Diagram 1

2 Sew a Template B triangle to one side of the Template A unit (Diagram 2). Stop sewing ¼ inch from the end of the seam, as shown.

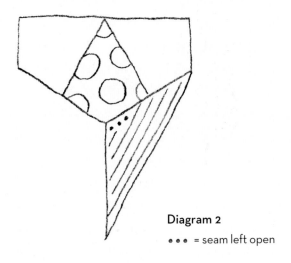

Diagram 2

• • • = seam left open

3 Sew a matching Template B triangle to the other side of the Template A unit. When you reach the Y junction of the seam, pivot on your needle and continue sewing out to the stem of the Y (Diagram 3). Press the seams under the green fabric.

4 Sew a Template C triangle to one side of the tulip and a matching Template C Reversed triangle to the other side (Diagram 4). Press the seams under the green fabric.

5 The finished blocks should measure 4¼ inches wide x 5 inches tall. Trim your blocks if necessary.

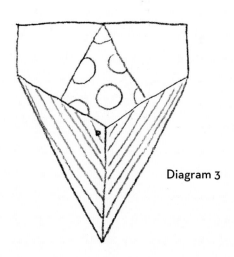

Diagram 3

6 Repeat Steps 1 to 5 to make a total of 93 Tulip blocks.

Assembling the blocks

If you did not try your hand at the *A Step Down* Dolly quilt before attempting this quilt, you will find that it is put together in an interesting manner. Due to the step-downs in the pattern, it cannot be sewn together in a straight line, or in rows. The easiest way to keep track of where you are up to is to lay the whole quilt out on a design wall or sheet so that you can pick up the pieces in order as you sew.

7 Referring to the photograph of the finished quilt, lay the Tulips and setting rectangles out according to the pattern. Don't worry too much about positioning until you have them all laid out, and then you can rearrange them until you are happy with the colour placement.

8 When you are pleased with the layout, begin sewing at the top left-hand corner. Sew setting rectangle A to the top edge of rectangle B (Diagram 5). Leave the end of the seam open by ½ inch, as shown. Turn the seam towards the setting rectangle.

9 Sew a setting rectangle D to the bottom of a Tulip block C, leaving the end of the seam open, as shown (Diagram 6). Now sew the first unit you created to the right-hand side of the Tulip C unit. Fold the seam towards the setting rectangle D.

10 Sew setting rectangle F to the side of Tulip block E, again leaving the seam open (Diagram 7). Turn the seam towards the setting rectangle and sew this unit to the unit above (Diagram 8).

11 Continue in this manner to expand the quilt. When you come to edges, trim the pieces to fit the space required and attach as above. This may seem a bit confusing, but the best way to understand it is to do it. You will find that after you have done a few open and

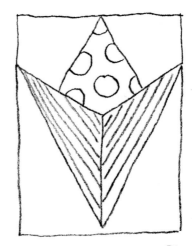

Diagram 4

• • • = seam left open

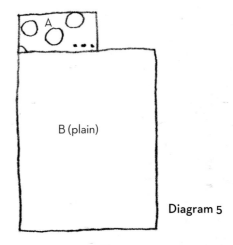

Diagram 5

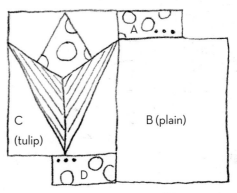

Diagram 6

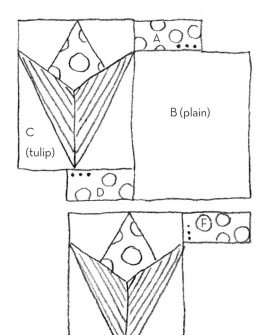

Diagram 7

• • • = seam left open

closed seams this way, you will be just fine. As long as you remember that the quilt cannot be put together in the usual rows, everything will be OK!

12 Continue until you have pieced all the Tulip blocks and rectangles together according to the photograph.

Borders

13 Sew all the 1½-inch border strips together, end to end, into one long strip. Press.

14 Ensure your quilt top is square and trim if it is not. Measure the quilt top through the centre across the middle of the quilt. Cut two pieces from the long strip to this measurement.

15 Find the centre of the top edge of the quilt top and the centre of one Border strip and pin. Pin the ends, then pin in between, easing if needed. Sew. Repeat with the bottom Border of the quilt.

16 Measure your quilt through the middle again, this time from top to bottom, and cut two strips to this measurement. Repeat Step 15 to attach the side Borders, as above. Press the border seams towards the border fabric. Your quilt top is complete.

{note on quilting}

I hand-quilted *The Night Garden* using a variety of different variegated perle cottons No 8. I outline-quilted all the tulips and quilted a tulip shape into the plain blocks. I then quilted a cross into the setting rectangles.

Backing, quilting and binding

Cut the backing fabric crosswise in half into two pieces, each 155 cm (63 inches) long. Remove the selvedges and stitch the pieces together up the long seams. Press the seam allowance open and press the backing piece carefully.

Refer to pages 190–199 for instructions on finishing.

Feathered blocks

Reflections in a Lake
Dolly quilt, 38 x 43 cm (15 x 17 inches)

Flock Together
Queen size, 234 cm (92 inches) square

Feathered Star quilts are notoriously difficult to put together, but piecing them is much easier if you first master the art of accurate half-square triangles on a small scale. Piecing the small units in the dolly quilt will help you to get your eye in and your accuracy levels up. Take care to carefully study the diagrams of the feathered stars before you begin. You might also find that making the *A Step Down* dolly quilt (on page 150) will also help you to practise piecing this quilt together, as there is an open seam technique there as well.

Reflections in a Lake

The Delectable Mountains blocks in this quilt seem to be reflected in the water. To achieve this effect, you need to make sure that you choose your fabrics carefully, so that the mountains are a deeper shade than the reflections. This quilt would make a beautiful bed-sized quilt as well; you need only expand the blocks across and down until the quilt is the right width and length.

These mountains are being reflected at sunset—you might want to try a green mountain in a blue summer lake, or snowy mountains in the winter. It would be interesting to make this quilt a night time scene also—imagine white mountains reflected in the moonlight on an ice blue lake. The possibilities are endless.

Degree of difficulty ✳✳✳

Finished quilt size

Dolly quilt, 38 x 43 cm (15 x 17 inches)

MATERIALS AND TOOLS

- 15 cm (6 inches) medium-pink fabric
- 15 cm (6 inches) light-pink fabric
- 5 cm (2 inches) blue-patterned fabric for water
- 20 cm (8 inches) light-blue fabric for background
- 15 cm (6 inches) dark-pink fabric for binding
- 1 fat quarter for backing fabric

- 45 x 50 cm (18 x 20 inches) cotton batting
- Sharp 2B pencil
- Template plastic
- Half-square triangle ruler (optional, see page 24)
- General sewing and patchwork supplies (see page 22)

TEMPLATES

Trace Templates A, B , C and D (on pattern sheet) onto template plastic with a sharp 2B pencil and cut out accurately using sharp scissors.

CUTTING

All fabrics are strip-cut across the width of the fabric from fold to selvedge unless otherwise specified or unless you are using a directional print.

FROM MEDIUM-PINK FABRIC, CUT:

- One strip, $1\frac{1}{2}$ inches wide. Cross-cut this strip into 32 half-square triangles, using Template A, or your half-square ruler.
- One strip, $2\frac{3}{4}$ inches wide. Cut this strip into four quarter-square triangles using Template B.

FROM LIGHT-PINK FABRIC, CUT:

- One strip $1\frac{1}{2}$ inches wide. Cross-cut this strip into 32 half-square triangles, using Template A, or your half-square ruler.
- One strip, $2\frac{3}{4}$ inches wide. Cut this strip into four quarter-square triangles using Template B.

FROM LIGHT-BLUE FABRIC, CUT:

- Two strips, $1\frac{1}{2}$ inches wide. Cross-cut these strips into 48 half-square triangles using Template A, or your half-square ruler. From the remaining fabric in the strips, cut four squares, each $1\frac{1}{2}$ inches.
- One strip, $4\frac{1}{4}$ inches wide. Cut this strip into four Template C quarter-square triangles and eight Template D half-square triangles.

FROM BLUE-PATTERNED 'WATER' FABRIC, CUT:

- One strip, $1\frac{1}{2}$ inches wide. (Strip will be trimmed to length during construction.)

FROM DARK-PINK FABRIC, CUT:

- Two strips, 3 inches wide. Set aside for binding.

Constructing the quilt top

1 Sew 24 of each of the medium-pink and light-pink Template A half-square triangles to a light blue Template A half-square triangle to make 48 squares in total (Diagram 1). Trim off the ears and finger-press the seam towards the pink fabrics.

2 Using the photograph as a guide, sew three of the medium-pink/blue squares together, with the pink diagonals all pointing in the direction shown (Diagram 2). Make four of these units. Make another four medium-pink/blue units with the diagonals pointing in the opposite direction (eight units in total).

3 Repeat Step 2 with the light-pink/blue squares to make another eight units.

4 Sew a pink half-square triangle (in the appropriate colourway) to the end of each strip (Diagram 3).

5 Sew a medium-pink triangle strip to the left-hand side of a medium-pink Template B quarter-square triangle (Diagram 4). Repeat with the remaining three medium-pink Template B quarter-square triangles.

6 Repeat Step 5 for the light-pink triangle strips and Template B quarter-square triangles.

Diagram 1

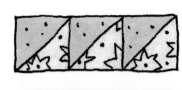

Diagram 2

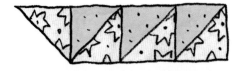
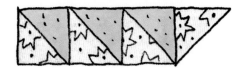

Diagram 3

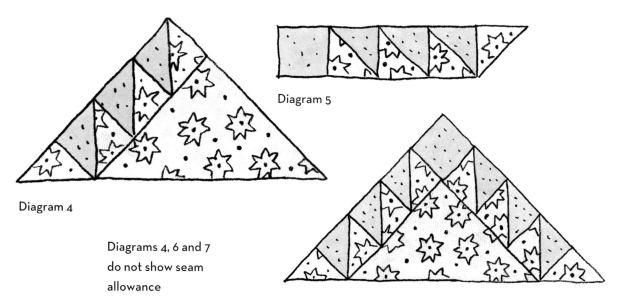

Diagram 4

Diagrams 4, 6 and 7
do not show seam
allowance

Diagram 5

Diagram 6

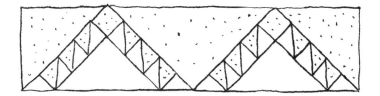

Diagram 7

7 Sew a blue 1½-inch square to the end of the remaining pink triangle strips in each colourway (Diagram 5).

8 Keeping the colourway sequence correct, sew these triangle strips to the right-hand side of the Template B quarter-square triangles (Diagram 6). Press.

9 Using the photograph of the quilt and Diagram 7 as a guide, sew a Template D half-square triangle to a medium-pink triangle unit, then a Template C quarter-square triangle, then another medium-pink triangle unit, and finally, another Template D half-square triangle. Press. Make another row identical to this one.

10 Repeat Step 9 for the light-pink triangle units, taking note of the positioning of the half-square and quarter-square triangles in each row. Press.

11 Measure your triangle rows through the centre and make sure they are straight. Trim if they are not. Cut two strips from the piece of blue water fabric to the length of your triangle row measurement.

12 Find the centre of Row 1 and the centre of a water strip. Pin the centres together, pin the ends, then pin in between, easing as you go if needed. Sew as pinned. Sew the next row to the lower edge of the water strip in the same way.

13 Sew a second water strip between Rows 3 and 4 in the same way, then sew the two sections together to assemble the quilt top. Your quilt top is complete.

Backing, quilting and binding

Using masking tape, tape the backing fabric, face down, onto a table, smoothing out any creases as you go. Lay the batting piece onto the backing, and then the quilt top on top. Smooth any creases and hand-baste the three layers together using large stitches and working from the centre out. As this is only a small quilt, it does not need a lot of basting. The backing and batting should be larger than the top for ease of quilting; don't be tempted to trim them back.

Refer to pages 190–199 for instructions on finishing.

{note on quilting}

I machine-quilted *Reflections in a Lake* in the ditch, using white cotton.

Flock Together

It's funny how things come together sometimes. I had been given a wonderful piece of red Vietnamese floral fabric by a friend, and I wanted it to become something spectacular as it was so beautiful. It was sitting on my bench in the studio to 'percolate' (I often leave things I want to work with lying around so I can see them), when a package arrived from South Africa. It had in it some amazing hand-stamped fabric that had caught my eye on Etsy. The two fell together, and when I added a box of Kaffe Fassett fat eighths I had been given at a show some months previously, I was in love!

Finished quilt size

Queen size, 234 cm (92 inches) square

Degree of difficulty
****

MATERIALS AND TOOLS

- 90 cm (1 yard) each of nine different white fabrics for backgrounds (see Note (a), opposite)

- 50 cm (20 inches) each of nine different bold red fabrics for stars

- 10 cm (4 inches) each of 45 different brightly-coloured fabrics for star points (see Note (b), opposite)

- 10 cm (4 inches) spotted blue fabric for the cornerstones

- 90 cm (1 yard) black-striped fabric for binding

- 8 m (8¾ yards) backing fabric

- 2.8 m (3 yards) square cotton batting

- Half-square triangle ruler (optional, see page 24)

- General sewing and patchwork supplies (see page 22)

{note}

(a) All my fabrics had either a red or a blue print on a white background. Be sure that the fabrics have enough contrast with the star points.

(b) I used a fat eighth pack of a Kaffe Fassett range—each pattern is a different group of star points. There are five different colourways of the same print in each star, 45 different fabrics in all. You can use larger amounts of fewer prints than this if you wish.

TEMPLATE

Trace Template A (on pattern sheet) onto template plastic with a sharp 2B pencil and cut out accurately using sharp scissors. (If you prefer, you can also use the 45-degree line on your patchwork ruler instead of a template to cut the diamonds.)

CUTTING

All fabrics are strip-cut across the width of the fabric from fold to selvedge unless otherwise specified or unless you are using a directional print.

FROM EACH OF THE NINE WHITE BACKGROUND FABRICS, CUT:

- One strip, $15\frac{1}{2}$ inches wide. From this strip, cross-cut one square $15\frac{1}{2}$ inches. Cut this square on both diagonals to yield four quarter-square triangles (36 quarter-square triangles in total).
- One strip, $8\frac{1}{2}$ inches wide. From this strip, cross-cut four squares, each $8\frac{1}{2}$ inches (36 squares in total).
- Six strips, $1\frac{7}{8}$ inches wide. From these strips, cross-cut 60 squares, each $1\frac{7}{8}$ inches. Cross-cut these squares on one diagonal to yield 120 half-square triangles per star (1,080 half-square triangles in total). Alternatively, you can cut your strips $1\frac{1}{2}$ inches wide and use the half-square triangle ruler to cut 120 half-square triangles per star.

FROM EACH OF THE NINE RED STAR FABRICS, CUT:

- One strip, $11\frac{7}{8}$ inches wide. From this strip, cut one square, $11\frac{7}{8}$ inches (nine squares in total).
- One strip, $7\frac{3}{8}$ inches wide. Cross-cut this strip into four squares, each $7\frac{3}{8}$ inches. Cross-cut these squares on one diagonal to yield eight half-square triangles (72 half-square triangles in total). Alternatively, cut your strip 7 inches wide and use the half-square triangle ruler to cut these triangles.

FROM EACH OF THE BRIGHT FABRICS, CUT:

- One strip, 1⅞ inches wide. Cross-cut these strips to yield 11 squares, each 1⅞ inches. Cross-cut these squares on one diagonal to yield 22 half-square triangles from each strip (990 triangles in total). You will need 104 triangles per star, or 936 triangles in total. Alternatively, cut your strips 1½ inches wide and use the half-square triangle ruler to cut 936 half-square triangles.
- One strip, 2 inches wide. Cross-cut these strips into 2-inch squares. You will need a total of 456 squares for the sashing and border (or 10 squares from each fabric, plus six extra).

From the remaining fabric, using Template A or the 45-degree line on your patchwork ruler, cut eight different patterned diamonds for each star, each 1½ inches wide with 2-inch long sides (a total of 72 diamonds).

FROM SPOTTED BLUE FABRIC, CUT:

- One strip, 2 inches wide. Cross-cut this strip to yield 16 squares, each 2 inches, for the cornerstones.

FROM BLACK-STRIPED FABRIC, CUT:

- 11 strips, 3 inches wide, for binding.

Constructing the quilt top

Feathered star blocks (make nine)

Before you start, it is a good idea to separate out all the pieces that you need for each of the nine complete star blocks. For each star block, you will need: one red square and eight red half-square triangles (all from the same fabric); four white background squares, four quarter-square triangles and 120 small half-square triangles (all from the same fabric); eight Template A diamonds (from random brights); and 104 small half-

square triangles (from random brights). Work on one block at a time, as follows:

1 Begin by sewing a white half-square triangle to each of the 104 coloured half-square triangles to form 104 squares. Carefully press the seams towards the coloured triangles. These are very small pieces, so make sure to simply press them, rather than moving the iron back and forth.

2 Lay all the pieces for one star out on a design wall or large piece of flannel or batting. Each star takes quite a while to make and it is easy to get confused about what goes where. Taking careful note of the direction of each triangle and diamond when you are laying out will save you the heartache of unpicking later on! Use Diagram 16 on page 179 as a guide: this will be simpler than trying to pick out all the little pieces in the photograph of the quilt.

3 Referring to Diagram 1, sew together a strip of five squares, with the triangles all facing in the correct direction. Add a white half-square triangle at the top of the strip, as shown. This is unit A1. Make four of these units. Press and return to the design wall.

4 Referring to Diagram 2, sew together a strip of five squares with the triangles all facing in the other direction. Add another square at the bottom (note the direction of the triangles) and a white half-square triangle at the top, as shown. This is unit A2. Make four of these units. Press and return to the design wall.

5 Referring to Diagram 3, sew together a strip of seven squares, with the triangles all facing the correct direction. Add a white half-square triangle and a Template A diamond at the top, as shown. This is unit A3. Make four of these units. Press and return to the design wall.

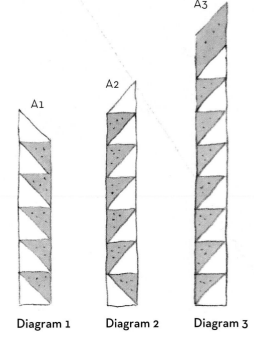

Diagram 1   **Diagram 2**   **Diagram 3**

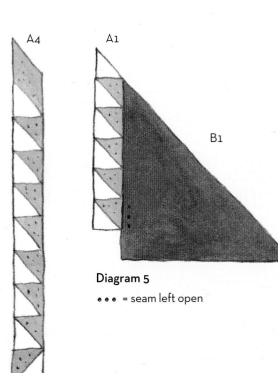

Diagram 4

Diagram 5

••• = seam left open

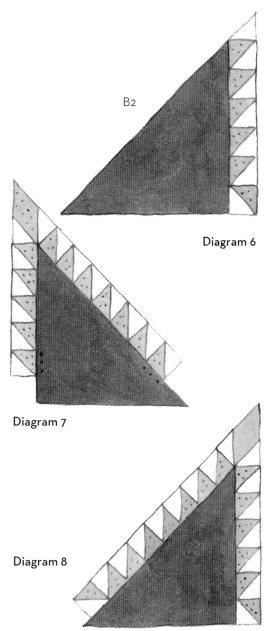

B2

Diagram 6

Diagram 7

Diagram 8

● ● ● = seam left open

6 Referring to Diagram 4, sew together a strip of seven squares, with the triangles all facing in the other direction. Add a white half-square triangle and a Template A diamond at the top and another square at the bottom (note the direction of the triangles). This is unit A4. Make four of these units. Press and return to the design wall.

7 Next, sew an A1 unit to the straight side of a red half-square triangle with a left-facing diagonal (Diagram 5). Leave at least 1 inch of the seam open at the bottom, as indicated. This is unit B1. Press.

8 Now sew an A2 unit to the straight side of a red half-square triangle with a right-facing diagonal (Diagram 6). The A2 unit is longer and will reach all the way to the bottom of the triangle. Sew to the end of the seam. This is unit B2. Press.

9 Referring to Diagram 7, sew an A3 unit to the diagonal edge of the B1 unit, taking care to match the seams at the point of the diamond. This strip will not reach the end of the large triangle, and you should again leave the seam open by at least 1 inch at the lower edge, as shown. Press.

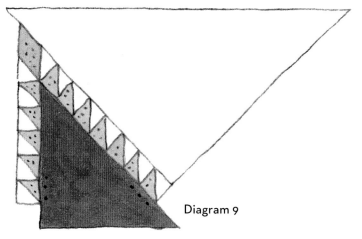

Diagram 9

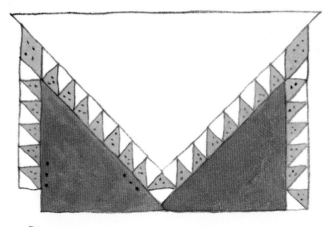

Diagram 10

... = seam left open

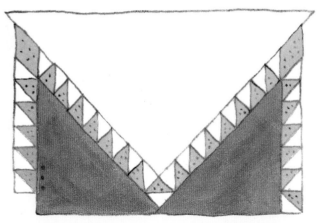

Diagram 11

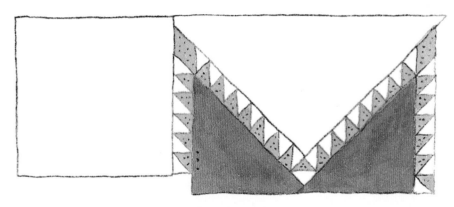

Diagram 12

10 Referring to Diagram 8, sew an A4 unit to the diagonal edge of the B2 unit, taking care to match the seams at the point of the diamond. Sew the seam all the way along. Press.

11 Referring to Diagram 9, take a large white background quarter-square triangle and sew the B1 unit to one of the short sides, as shown. Press.

12 Sew the B2 unit to the other side of the triangle. The B2 unit will reach all the way along the triangle and match with the end of the B1 unit (Diagram 10).

13 Close the seam on the B1 unit (Diagram 11). Press.

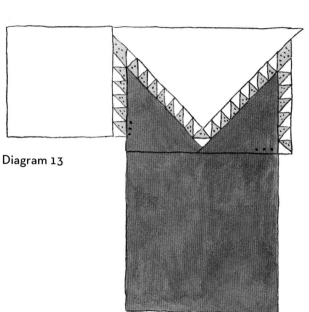

Diagram 13

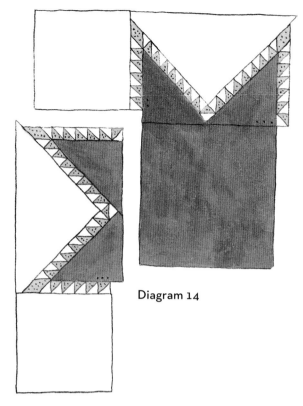

Diagram 14

Diagram 15

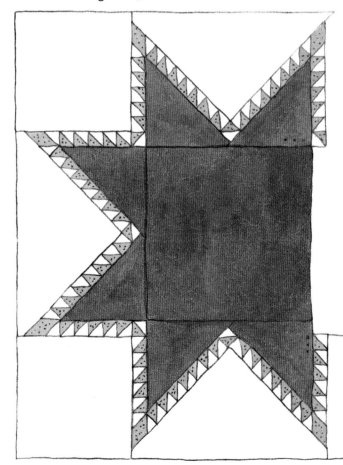

• • • = seam left open

14 Next, sew an 8½-inch white background square to the short side of all four B1 units to make four star-point strips (Diagram 12). Press.

15 Find the centre of one edge of the centre red square and finger-press a crease. Match this crease with the centre of one star-point strip and sew the two together (Diagram 13). Leave the end of the seam open at the B2 unit end of the seam by at least 1 inch. Do not press at this stage, until you have finished the whole block.

Diagram 16

16 If you have not already done so, return all the pieces to the design wall to check placement and orientation. Referring to Diagram 14, sew another star-point strip to the next side of the red square. First, join the seam of the B2 unit to the white background square, then sew the triangles along the centre square, closing the seam on the B1 unit as you do so.

17 Turn the unit to the next side and join another star-point strip as before, closing the seam again as shown in Diagram 15.

18 Join the last star-point strip to the centre square, closing all the seams as you do so, as shown in Diagram 16. Press the block and check that it is square, trimming if it is not.

Sashing

19 Take the 2-inch bright sashing squares and sew them randomly together into 24 strips of 19 squares each. Press. Set aside 12 strips.

20 Take the remaining 12 sashing strips and sew together four long rows of sashing, beginning and ending with a spotted blue square cornerstone. Each row should have three sashing strips with a spotted blue square in between, and at each end. Press.

{note on quilting}
I had *Flock Together* machine-quilted by Kim Bradley in a large all-over floral pattern, in white cotton.

Assembling the quilt top

21 Using the photograph of the quilt as a guide, sew together three rows of Feathered Star blocks, beginning and ending with a 19-square sashing strip and with a sashing strip in between each block. Press.

22 Starting and finishing with a long row of sashing, assemble the quilt in rows, with a long row of sashing between each row. Take care to match all the seams and pin where needed. Press. Your quilt top is complete.

Backing, quilting and binding

Cut the backing fabric crosswise, giving three pieces, each 266 cm (105 inches) long. Remove the selvedges and stitch the pieces together up the middle seams. Press the seam allowance open and press the backing piece carefully.

Refer to pages 190–199 for instructions on finishing.

Basics, layout and assembly

Quilt basics

Sewing techniques

Foundation piecing

Foundation piecing is a clever technique, used to make blocks of exactly the same size, to achieve accurate designs with sharp points or to stabilise scraps and control bias stretching.

It involves, as the name implies, the use of paper or fabric as a base, or foundation, for piecing. Lines drawn on the underside of the foundation allow straight accurate seams that make even the most advanced blocks able to be sewn perfectly.

Foundation papers can be purchased in quilt or craft shops. The block designs need to be traced or copied onto the papers, so you will need at least one page per block. Be sure to choose a paper that feeds into your printer or photocopier. In some cases, it is possible to use standard copier paper. However, if seams intersect, this is not such a good option. The paper gets removed once the blocks are sewn and this task can be tedious if the paper cannot be removed easily.

The first step is to trace or copy the pattern for the desired number of blocks onto the foundation paper (Picture 1). Set your sewing machine to a small stitch, say 1.5, which helps when the time comes to remove the papers later. Sewing through the paper will dull your needle, so remember to change to a fresh needle when doing other sewing.

The fabrics need to be placed right sides together with the paper, right side up, on top (Picture 2). Hold the paper up to a light to be sure that the fabric covers the necessary area. Be aware of where the fabric will be sewn and make

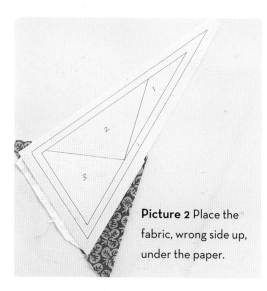

Picture 1 Trace onto the foundation paper.

Picture 2 Place the fabric, wrong side up, under the paper.

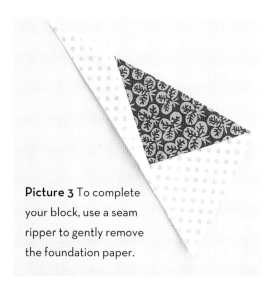

Picture 3 To complete your block, use a seam ripper to gently remove the foundation paper.

sure that it covers the next seam line when pressed flat. Sew the line, trim off the excess seam allowance, then flip the strip and press in place. Be sure to leave a $1/4$-inch seam allowance on the last strip.

When the block is completely stitched, fold over the first strip at the seam and finger-press along the sewing line. Use a seam ripper to gently help loosen the paper. Do not rip out the paper or the stitches will loosen (Picture 3).

Appliqué

There are various appliqué techniques, but my favourite is the needle-turn methodS, described below. Whatever appliqué method you choose, complete all the appliqué before piecing the blocks together, unless otherwise instructed.

Before beginning the appliqué, decide where you want your shapes to sit on the background block. Use a sharp 2B pencil or other marker to lightly trace the shapes onto the background fabric. A light box is useful when tracing; if you don't have one, tape the design to be traced onto a sunny window, lightly tape the fabric over it, then trace the design.

Remember that some designs will need to have their various elements sewn down in a particular order. For example, when sewing a flower, the stem will need to be sewn first so that it sits under the flower petals, then the petals added, and lastly the flower centre and the leaves. If you are working on a complicated appliqué design and you think you might get confused, draw or photocopy a diagram of the complete design, determine the order in which the pieces need to be laid down, and then number the shapes on the diagram so you can keep track.

Needle-turn appliqué

Trace the template shapes onto template plastic or cardboard using a sharp 2B pencil. Using paper scissors (not your fabric scissors), cut out along the traced line.

Place the template on the right side of the fabric and trace around it. I use a silver gel pen for marking my sewing lines, firstly, because it's reflective and shows up on any fabric, and secondly, because it's really easy to see whether or not you have turned your shape under neatly or not. If you can still see silver, you haven't got the shape right! However, gel pen does not wash off. Once you have traced your shape onto the fabric, you're married to it, so be careful with that tracing!

Trace the shape you are going to appliqué onto the right side of the fabric with the gel pen, taking care to leave space between the pieces for a seam allowance. Cut the shapes out a scant $1/4$ inch from the gel line. Finger-press along the line all around the shape, including into any curves or points. Do not be tempted to iron the press in. A finger-pressed line is easy to manipulate, whereas an ironed line is difficult to change if you iron a point into a crease or a line in the wrong spot. You will also be very likely to burn your fingers!

Position the pieces on the background block using the traced outline or photograph supplied with the pattern as a guide. Note which parts of the pieces may go under others; dotted lines on the template pieces indicate which parts of each piece should be placed under adjacent pieces.

Instead of pins, I use appliqué glue to fix the pieces temporarily onto the background. You can glue all the appliqué shapes onto a quilt and carry it around with you, without worrying that the pins have come out. You only need a few dots of glue on each shape to make them stick. Leave for a few minutes for the glue to dry. Don't worry if the glue smudges, as it is easily peeled back later or washed off.

Thread your appliqué needle with thread to match the appliqué fabric. You should always match your appliqué thread to the colour of the fabric shape that you are

Tracing the outlines lightly onto the background fabric will help to position the shapes.

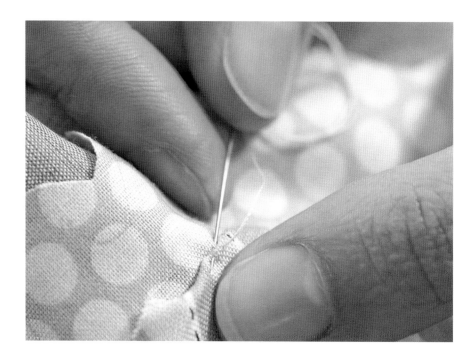

Picture 1 Run your needle along underneath the background and come up again right on the edge of the appliqué shape.

Picture 2 Your stitches should just catch the edge of the fabric and be quite small and close together.

appliquéing, not to the background. I use very long, fine straw needles for appliqué: the finer the needle, the smaller you can make your stitches for invisible appliqué. You can start anywhere, but try to never start on an inside curve.

Tie a knot in the thread and come up from the back to the front of the quilt, catching the very edge of the fabric with your needle. Go down into the background fabric right next to where you came up, run your needle along underneath the background and come up again right on the edge of the appliqué shape (Picture 1). Don't try to turn the whole edge under before you sew it; just turn under the small section you are working on. This makes it easier to keep track of the gel pen line and make sure that you turn it all under.

Sew all around the cut edge in this manner. Your stitches should just catch the edge of the fabric and be quite small and close together, which will make the appliqué strong and avoid its being torn or looking puckered (Picture 2).

The best way to get a sharp point is this: sew all the way up to the point on one side. Fold the fabric down 90 degrees under the point, then sweep the remaining fabric downwards and underneath the main part of the point.

Picture 3 You will need to clip in all the way to the seam line on an inside point.

Take a stitch right at the point again and give it a sharp tug, then continue sewing down the other side of the point.

When you get to an inside curve, you've reached your next challenge! You can sew all around the outside curves without clipping, but inside curves needs clipping (Picture 3). Using very sharp, small scissors, carefully clip in to the silver line, about $1/4$ inch apart, all around the inner curve.

I never clip anything until I am ready to sew it. If you do, it can fray and get messy. Sew all the way up to the curve before you clip, and then sew the curve right away.

Continue until you have sewn all around the outside of the shape and tie the thread off at the back with a small knot.

Turn the block over and make a small cut at the back of the shape, taking care not to cut the appliqué. Cut the background away underneath the appliqué. Be sure not to cut closer than $1/4$ inch away from the seam lines. Although it is not necessary, removing the fabric in this way makes the appliqué sit nicely and creates fewer layers to quilt through, especially where appliqué pieces overlap.Repeat this process with each shape. Remove the background from under each piece before applying the next one (Picture 4).

Picture 4 To reduce bulk, cut the background away beneath the appliqué.

Quilt layout and assembly

Constructing your quilt

If a layout diagram is given, be sure to refer to it as well as the photograph. Many quilt designs, especially complex ones using more than one type of block, feature optical illusions caused by the way in which the various components are combined. Sometimes the logic of the quilt's construction will not become clear until you look at a layout diagram.

Adding borders

Borders may be added for decorative effect, to increase the quilt's size, or both. They may have squared-off or mitred corners. The quilt pattern will tell you what length to cut the borders, but you should always measure your quilt before cutting the border fabric, then adjust the length of the border strips if necessary.

Measure in both directions through the middle of the quilt rather than along the edges. This is because the edges may have distorted a little during the making of the quilt, especially if any of the edge pieces are bias cut. Use these measurements to calculate the length of each border.

If adding squared-off borders, the side borders will be the length of the quilt top. The top and bottom borders will be the width of the quilt top with the side borders added. Unless a pattern indicates otherwise, sew the side borders on first, press the seams towards the border, then add the top and bottom borders.

If adding borders with mitred corners, each border will need to be the width or length of the quilt, plus twice the width of the border, to allow enough fabric for mitring, plus seam allowance. Sew each border to the edge of the quilt,

beginning and ending the seam a precise $^1/_4$ inch (6 mm) from the edge of the quilt. Fold the quilt so that the side and the top are flush and the two border strips extend to the side. Use your ruler and a 45-degree-angle line to mark a line from the $^1/_4$-inch point to the edge of the strip. Sew along this line and check before cutting—it must lie flat. When confident, trim off the extra and repeat for all four corners.

Layering the quilt

Once you have added all the borders, and before you can begin quilting, you need to assemble or sandwich all three layers of the quilt.

The batting and backing should both be at least 4 inches (10 cm) larger all round than the quilt top. You may need to join two widths of fabric, or add a strip of scraps or leftover blocks, to obtain a large enough piece for the backing.

Press the quilt top and backing. Lay the backing right side down on a large, flat, clean surface (preferably one that is not carpeted), smooth it out carefully, then tape it to the surface using masking tape. Tape it at intervals along all

Sandwich the batting between
the quilt top and the backing.

sides, but do not tape the corners, as this will cause the bias to stretch out of shape.

Place the batting on top of the backing and smooth it out. If you need to join two pieces of batting, butt them up together and machine-zigzag a seam.

On top of the batting, place the well-pressed quilt top, right side up, ensuring that the top and backing are square to each other. Smooth it out.

The three layers must now be basted together ready for quilting.

Basting

Basting can be done with safety pins or long hand-stitches.

If using safety pins, start from the centre of the quilt and pin through all three layers at intervals of about 8 inches (20 cm). If you are intending to machine-quilt, make sure the pins are kept away from the lines to be quilted. Once the whole quilt is safety-pinned, it can be moved.

If you are intending to hand-quilt, baste the whole quilt both horizontally and vertically, always working from the centre out, using long hand-stitches at intervals of about 6 inches (15 cm). Using a curved needle is a good idea, as this makes the task easier on the wrists.

Do not baste using hand-stitches if you intend to machine-quilt, as the basting threads will get caught under the presser foot. Do not use safety pins if you are hand-quilting as the pins prevent the hoop from sitting evenly.

Some quilting stores offer a machine-basting service. This can be a worthwhile investment, especially if you are going to be doing fine hand-quilting in the traditional manner, a task that can take months or even years.

Remove the basting stitches or safety pins only once all the quilting is complete.

{note}

TYPES OF BATTING

Some battings need to be quilted closer together than others to stop them from drifting around within the quilt or fragmenting when washed. Polyester batting requires less quilting than cotton or wool batting. However, some polyester battings have a tendency to fight the sewing machine.

Wool battings (usually actually a wool/polyester or a wool/cotton blend) provide more warmth and comfort than polyester battings. However, they require more quilting, and those that are not needle-punched tend to pill. Needle-punched wool blends are more stable and require less quilting. Traditional cotton battings require a lot of quilting, as much as every $1/2$–3 inches (12–75 mm). Needle-punched cotton batting are more stable and can be quilted up to 10 inches (25 cm) apart. Ask your quilt store for advice if you are unsure of what to choose.

FINISHING A THREAD

Hold the thread out to the side with your left hand, and loop a one-loop knot using the needle (Picture A, page 196). Slide the loose knot down the thread until it lies directly on the quilt top, and tighten the knot (Picture B, page 196). Take the needle back down through the hole the thread is coming out of and slide it away through the batting. Bring the needle back up to the top of the quilt and give the thread a tug. The knot will follow down into the hole and lodge in the batting. Cut the thread close to the surface (Picture C, page 197).

Picture 1 Use a thimble to push the needle through the three layes of the quilt.

Quilting

Quilting can be fairly rudimentary, its main purpose being to hold together the layers of the quilt, or it can be decorative and sometimes extremely elaborate. Machine-quilting is quick, but nothing beats hand-quilting for sheer heirloom beauty.

Designs for hand-quilting, or elaborate designs for machine-quilting, are generally marked on the quilt top before the quilt's layers are sandwiched together. On pale fabrics, the marking is done lightly in pencil; on dark fabrics, use a special quilter's silver pencil. Pencil lines can be erased later.

If you intend to quilt straight lines or a cross-hatched design, masking tape can be used to mark out the lines on the quilt top. Such tape comes in various widths, from 1/4 inch upwards. Free-flowing lines can be drawn on with a chalk pencil.

If you intend to outline-quilt by machine, you may be able to sew straight enough lines by eye; if not, you will need to mark the quilt top first.

Hand-quilting

Quilting by hand produces a softer line than machine-quilting and will give an heirloom quality to quilts. Most of the quilts in this book are quilted using perle cotton, since it is often easier for beginners to work with and stands out vividly against the fabric's surface, although traditional quilting thread can be used if you prefer.

To quilt by hand, the fabric needs to be held in a frame (also known as a quilting hoop). Free-standing frames are available, but hand-held ones are cheaper, more portable and just as effective. One edge of a hand-held frame can be leaned against a table or bench to enable you to keep both hands free.

Hand-quilting, like machine-quilting, should commence in the centre of the quilt and proceed outwards. To commence hand-quilting, place the plain (inner) ring of the frame under the centre of the quilt. Position the other

Picture 2 Put your thumb in front of the needle while pushing from the back.

ring, with the screw, over the top of the quilt to align with the inner ring. Tighten the screw so that the fabric in the frame becomes firm, but not drum-tight.

For traditional quilting, choose the smallest needle that you feel comfortable with. (These needles are known as 'betweens'.) For quilting with perle cotton, use a good-quality crewel embroidery needle (I use a No 9). Thread the needle with about 18 inches (45 cm) of thread. Knot the end of the thread with a one-loop knot and take the needle down through the quilt top into the batting, a short distance from where you want to start quilting. Tug the thread slightly so that the knot pulls through into the batting, making the starting point invisible. Proceed as follows.

The hand-quilting action With your dominant hand above the quilt and the other beneath, insert the needle through all three layers at a time, with the middle or index finger of your dominant hand (use a metal thimble to make this easier) until you can feel the tip of the needle resting on your finger at the back (Picture 1). Without pushing the

Picture A (top) Hold the thread out to the side and loop a one-loop knot using the needle.

Picture B (bottom) Slide the loose knot down the thread until it lies directly on the quilt top, and tighten the knot.

needle through, rock the needle back to the top of the quilt and use your underneath finger to push the tip of the needle up. Put your upper thumb down in front of the needle tip while pushing up from the back (Picture 2). This will make a small 'hill' in the fabric. Push the needle through the fabric. This makes one stitch. To take several stitches at once, push the needle along to the required stitch length then dip the tip into the fabric and repeat the above technique. Gently pull the stitches to indent the stitch line evenly. You should always quilt toward yourself, as this reduces hand and shoulder strain, so turn the quilt in the required direction. You can protect your underneath finger using a stick-on plastic shield such as a Thimble-It. You can also use a leather thimble: however, this does make it more difficult to feel how far the needle has come through, and thus more difficult to keep your stitches even.

To move a short distance from one part of the quilting design to another, push the tip of the needle through the batting and up at the new starting point. Take care not to drag a dark thread under a light fabric, as the line will show.

When you come to the edge of the hoop, leave the thread dangling so that you can pick it up and continue working with it once you have repositioned the hoop. Work all the quilting design within the hoop before repositioning the hoop and beginning to quilt another area. If you need to quilt right up to the border edge, baste lengths of spare cotton fabric to the edge of the quilt, thus giving you enough fabric area to position the edges of the quilt under the quilting hoop.

To fasten off a length of thread, see page 194.

Machine-quilting

You may want to machine-quilt your quilt yourself, but I use and recommend a professional quilting service for a couple of good reasons.

Firstly, finished quilts are usually quite large and, consequently, rather cumbersome. It really is a fairly tricky job to manipulate the bulk of the quilt on a domestic sewing machine, even using a specialised walking foot. Having pieced your precious quilt so carefully, it would be a shame to spoil it now with puckers and distortions.

Secondly, professional machine-quilters offer a large range of quilting patterns to suit every need and taste and can also advise you on a design that will enhance all your careful work.

Picture C Cut the thread close to the surface.

Binding

From the width of the binding fabric, cut enough strips of fabric to equal the outside edge of your quilt, plus about 6 inches (15 cm) to allow for mitred corners and for the ends to be folded under. I cut my binding strips 3 inches wide and use a $1/2$-inch seam when attaching them to the quilt.

Seam the strips into a continuous length, making the joins at 45-degree angles as shown on page 199. To do this, fold under one end at a 45-degree angle and finger-press a crease. Unfold. The crease line will become the seam line. Mark this line lightly with a pencil. With right sides together and the two fabric pieces at 90 degrees, align the angled cut end with another strip of binding fabric. Align the $1/4$-inch measurement on a quilter's ruler with this line and trim off the corner. Sew the two strips together along the marked line. Press all seams to one side and trim off the 'ears'.

Press the entire strip in half along its length. Doubling the fabric like this makes the binding more durable.

Trim the backing and the batting so that they are even with the edge of the quilt top. Beginning at one end of the binding strip, pin the binding to one edge of the quilt, starting about 4 inches (10 cm) in from a corner and having raw edges even. Attach a walking foot to your machine and machine-sew in place through all the layers of the quilt, using a $1/2$-inch seam allowance and mitring the corners. To mitre corners, end the seam $1/2$ inch from the corner and fasten off. Fold the binding fabric up at a 45-degree angle, then fold it down so that the fold is level with the

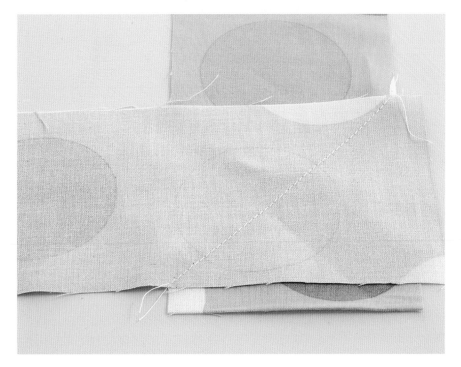

To create your binding, join the strips (left), trim the corners (below), and tuck the end of the binding under itself using a diagonal fold (bottom), which will become the seam line.

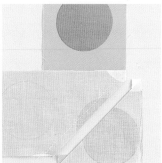

edge of the binding just sewn. Begin the next seam at the edge of the quilt and proceed as before. Repeat this process to mitre all the corners.

When you approach the point at which the binding started, trim the excess, tuck the end of the binding under itself using a diagonal fold and stitch the rest of the seam.

Press the binding away from the quilt. Turn the binding to the back of the quilt and blind hem-stitch in place by hand to finish. Your quilt is now complete!

Glossary

APPLIQUÉ A technique in which small pieces of fabric are stitched to a background fabric.

BACKING The undermost layer of a quilt.

BASTING A method of holding together several layers of fabric during quilting, so that they do not move around. Basting may be done using a long hand-stitch, or with safety pins. The stitches or pins are removed once the quilting is complete.

BATTING The middle layer of a quilt; also known as wadding.

BIAS The diagonal of a woven fabric, at a 45-degree angle to the straight grain (the warp and weft). Fabric cut on the bias stretches, so care must be taken when handling and sewing bias-cut pieces.

BINDING The narrow strips of fabric (usually made of a double thickness) that enclose the raw edges and batting of a quilt.

BLOCK The basic unit of a quilt top. Blocks are usually square, but may be rectangular, hexagonal or other shapes. They may be plain (of one fabric only), appliquéd or pieced.

BORDER A strip of fabric (plain, appliquéd or pieced) joined to the central panel of a quilt and used to frame it and also to add extra size.

CHAIN-PIECING A method of joining fabric pieces by machine in an assembly-line fashion, which speeds up the process and uses less thread. Pairs or sets of block pieces are fed into the machine, one after the other, without snipping the threads between them.

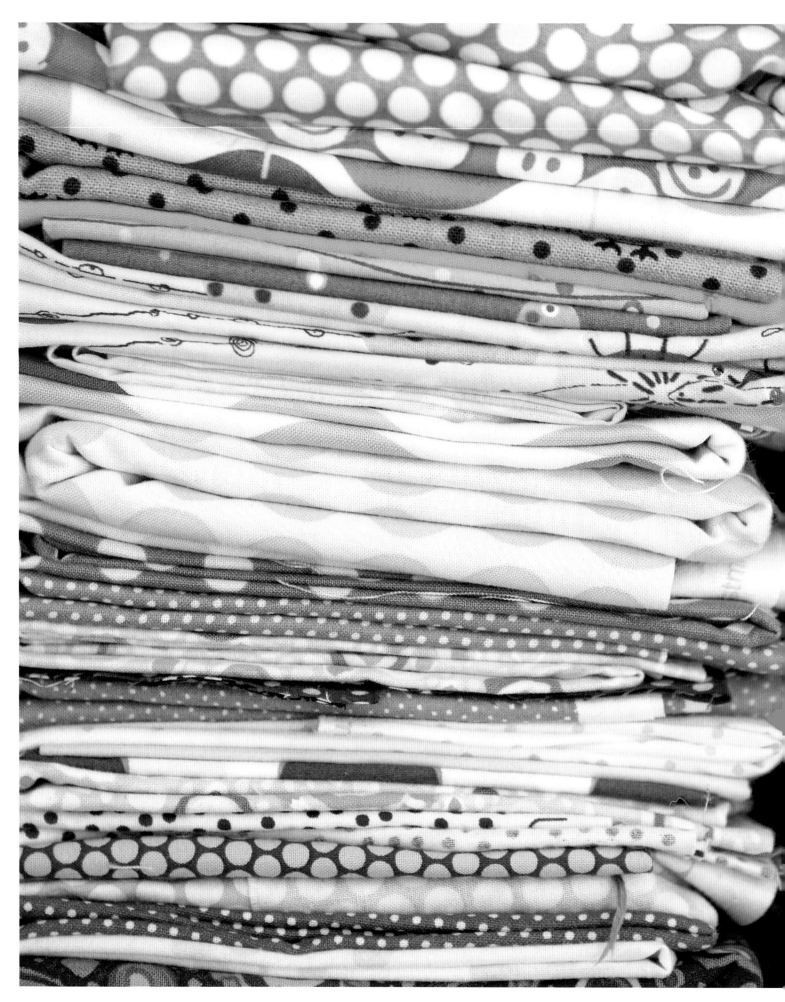

CROSS-HATCHING A quilting pattern of parallel equidistant lines that run in two directions to form a grid of squares or diamonds.

DIRECTIONAL PRINT Printed fabric in which there is a distinct direction to the pattern, whether straight or at an angle; for example, stripes, human or animal figures, or some florals.

EASE To make two pieces of fabric of different sizes fit together in the one seam. One piece may have to be stretched or gathered slightly to bring it to the required length. To ease, first pin the pieces at intervals until they fit, then sew them.

FAT QUARTER A piece of fabric that is made by cutting a metre or a yard of fabric in halves first vertically then horizontally. The piece thus cut is approximately 50 x 56 cm (in metric systems) or 18 x 22 inches (in imperial measurements).

FEED DOGS The teeth under the sewing plate of a sewing machine, which move to pull the fabric through the machine. The feed dogs must be lowered to allow for free-motion quilting.

FINGER-PRESSING A way of pressing a temporary crease in a piece of fabric, for example when finding the middle of two pieces so that they can be matched before being joined. Running a fingernail along a crease will make it lie flat.

GRAIN The direction of the fabric, along the warp (vertical threads) or the weft (horizontal threads). These are both straight grains, along which woven fabrics do not stretch. Compare with Bias.

HALF-SQUARE TRIANGLE A triangle that is made from a square cut across one diagonal. Half-square triangles have the bias along the hypotenuse (or longest side). Compare with Quarter-square triangle.

MITRED CORNER A corner that is joined at a 45-degree angle.

NOVELTY PRINT A fabric printed with themed designs, such as toys, cartoon characters or animals.

ON POINT An arrangement in which the quilt blocks are placed diamond-fashion, with their corners at the 12, 3, 6 and 9 o'clock positions, rather than in a square fashion.

OUTLINE-QUILT To make one or more outlines of a motif or block design, radiating outwards.

PATCHWORK A generic term for the process of sewing together many small pieces of fabric to make a quilt. Also known as piecework.

PIECE An individual fabric shape that may be joined to other fabric shapes to make a quilt block, or used on its own (in which case it is known as a one-patch). Also known as a patch.

PIECING The process of joining together pieces of fabric to make a quilt top, a quilt block or a border.

PIN-BASTE To pin through the layers of a quilt 'sandwich', using safety pins, to hold them together during quilting. The pins are removed once the quilting is complete.

QUARTER-SQUARE TRIANGLE A triangle that is made from a square, cut across both diagonals. Quarter-square triangles have the bias along the two short sides.

QUILT TOP The uppermost, decorative layer of a quilt. It may be pieced, appliquéd or a combination of both, with or without borders.

QUILTER'S RULERS Precision-cut, straight-edged plastic rulers in various sizes, used with rotary cutters and rotary-cutting (self-healing) mats. They make it easy to cut accurate shapes, and to cut through several layers of fabric at once. They come in straight varieties and also those designed for cutting at various angles or for creating triangles.

QUILTING In general, the process of making a quilt; more specifically, the process of stitching patterns by hand or machine into the quilt layers to decorate the quilt, add strength and anchor the batting inside the quilt.

QUILTING FRAME A free-standing floor apparatus, made of wood or plastic tubing, in which a quilt is held while it is being quilted.

QUILTING HOOP A hand-held circular wooden device in which a quilt is held while being quilted.

RAW EDGE The cut edge of a fabric.

ROTARY CUTTER A cutting device similar in appearance to a pizza cutter, with a razor-sharp circular blade. Used in conjunction with a quilter's ruler and quilting mat, it allows several layers of fabric to be cut at once, easily and with great accuracy.

ROTARY-CUTTING MAT A self-healing plastic mat on which rotary cutters are used. It protects both the blade of the cutter and the work surface beneath the mat.

SASHING Strips of fabric that separate blocks in a quilt, to frame them and/or make the quilt larger.

SEAM ALLOWANCE The margin of fabric between the cut edge and seam line. For quilting and most appliqué, it is ¼ inch.

SEAM LINE The guideline that is followed while sewing.

SELVEDGES The woven finished edges along the length of the fabric.

SETTING The way in which blocks are arranged in a quilt top, for example, square or on point.

SETTING SQUARE A plain block or square used with pieced or appliquéd blocks in a quilt top.

SETTING TRIANGLE A triangle placed between blocks along the side of a quilt set on point, to straighten up the edges.

STASH A quilter's hoard of fabrics.

TEMPLATE Plastic, cardboard or paper shape used for tracing and cutting fabric pieces for piecing or appliqué, or to transfer quilting designs to a quilt top.

WALKING FOOT A special sewing-machine foot that feeds the top layer of a quilt sandwich evenly through the machine, while the feed dogs control the bottom layer.

WARP The lengthwise threads in a woven fabric, which interlock with the weft threads. See also Weft.

WEFT The widthwise threads in a woven fabric, which interlock with the warp threads. See also Warp.

{acknowledgements}

Who to thank, who to thank...the list is long and distinguished, but as usual I will start with my wonderful, supportive and long suffering husband Damian, and my home-based fan club of Charlie and Oscar. My three boys make everything in life worthwhile. Thanks also to my Dad for his support through a crazy, crazy year.

Thank you to Kay, and to the marketing team at Murdoch Books for having the faith in me to go forward in a new venture. Your support means everything! Also at Murdoch thank you to Diana Hill, Vivien Valk and the team behind the scenes. Extra thanks to lovely Sophia Oravecz for putting up with my millions of emails and organising everything so wonderfully. Working with Murdoch Books is a fantastic experience, I always feel so involved with every aspect of the production of the book and I am so very grateful for that.

Huge thanks to my editor, Georgina Bitcon, for her incredible mathematical brain and her endless patience! Without Georgina you would all be making very strangely shaped quilts indeed.

I was very lucky to have the amaaaaaazing photography of Sue Stubbs, which has shown the quilts off so beautifully. Thanks Sue for being able to take such great pictures, even in my tiny little sewing room!

Thanks and kisses to Flo, Erica, Amy and Bee for champagne and chocolates, listening to my ramblings and giving me your fantastic friendships and your strong opinions. To my Wednesday Night Girls for sticking with me, even when I've been so tired I'm not much of a teacher!

To all my online friends near and far who read my blog, tweet me, read Sewn, buy my books and send me chatty, friendly emails. I love to hear from you all and enjoy seeing your quilts so much. Don't stop!

And lastly to my delicious little white dog, Madam, for being such a perfect cover girl. Well done Muttie, chicken for you.

{resources}

I'm aware that many people who buy my books are just starting out on their quilting journeys, so here are a few bits and pieces, interesting places to go and sites to shop at.

There are many wonderful bricks-and-mortar quilt shops in the world, and where possible I encourage you to shop at your local patchwork shop rather than buy online. I'm aware that this isn't always possible, but a local quilt shop will help you select your fabric, give you recommendations and hints, and offer great classes to help you along the way. Your local quilt shop can't survive to have your classes unless you also shop with them.

Obviously listing every quilt shop is not possible, so here are a few online shops (that ship worldwide!) I like to visit.

Fabric online

- CV Quiltworks www.cvquiltworks.com
- Fabricworm www.fabricworm.com
- Fat Quarter Shop
  www.fatquartershop.com
- Glorious Color www.gloriouscolor.com
- Pink Chalk Fabrics
  www.pinkchalkfabrics.com
- Hip Fabric www.hipfabric.com
- Sew Mama Sew www.sewmamasew.com
- Quilt Fabric Delights
  www.quiltfabricdelights.com

Notions online

- Matilda's Own Rulers: Oz Quilts
  www.ozquilts.com.au
- Matilda's Own www.matildasown.com
- Nifty Notions Rulers: The Quilters Store
  www.thequiltersstore.com.au
- Wilderness Road Quilt co
  www.wrqcd.com
- Kaye England www.kayeengland.com
- Applique Glue and Needles: Sue Daley
  www.patchworkwithbusyfingers.com

Websites for quilting information and industry news

- Craft Gossip www.craftgossip.com
- Fat Quarterly www.fatquarterly.com
- Sewn www.sewn.net.au
- True Up www.trueup.net
- Whip Up www.whipup.net

Inspirational blogs for quilts, fabrics and fun

- A Quilt is Nice
  www.aquiltisnice.blogspot.com
- Bemused www.bemused.typepad.com
- Glorious Applique
  www.gloriousapplique.blogspot.com
- I'm a Ginger Monkey
  www.imagingermonkey.blogspot.com
- Inspired by Antique Quilts
  www.inspiredbyantiquequilts.blogspot.com
- Mrs Schmenkman Quilts
  www.mrsschmenkmanquilts.wordpress.com
- One Flew Over
  www.oneflewover-oneflewover.com
- Pam Kitty Morning
  www.pamkittymorning.blogspot.com
- Red Pepper Quilts
  www.redpepperquilts.com
- The Happy Zombie
  www.thehappyzombie.com
- Wee Wonderfuls
  www.weewonderfuls.com

Sarah Fielke patterns, books, ruler sets and kits

- Sarah's blog www.thelastpiece.net
- Sarah's website www.sarahfielke.com
  or Google your nearest quilt shop!

Published in 2011 by Murdoch Books Pty Limited

Murdoch Books Australia
Pier 8/9
23 Hickson Road
Millers Point NSW 2000
Phone: +61 (0) 2 8220 2000
Fax: +61 (0) 2 8220 2558
www.murdochbooks.com.au

Murdoch Books UK Limited
Erico House, 6th Floor
93–99 Upper Richmond Road
Putney, London SW15 2TG
Phone: +44 (0) 20 8785 5995
Fax: +44 (0) 20 8785 5985
www.murdochbooks.co.uk

Publisher: Diana Hill
Photographer: Sue Stubbs
Editor: Georgina Bitcon
Project editor: Sophia Oravecz
Designer: Clare O'Loughlin

National Library of Australia Cataloguing-in-Publication Data

Author: Fielke, Sarah.
Title: Quilting : from little things / Sarah Fielke.
ISBN: 978-1-74196-760-9 (pbk.)
Subjects: Quilting
              Quilting--Patterns.
              Patchwork--Patterns.
              Patchwork quilts.

Dewey Number: 746.46

A catalogue record for this book is available from the British Library.

Printed by 1010 Printing International Limited, China

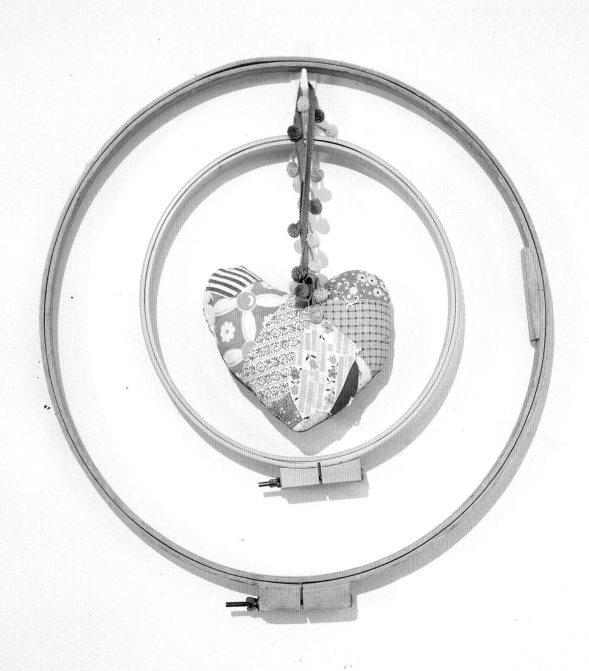